BROADWAY & HOLLYWOOD

BROADWAY & HOLLYWOOD

Costumes Designed by Irene Sharaff

Irene Sharaff

VNR VAN NOSTRAND REINHOLD COMPANY
New York Cincinnati Toronto London Melbourne

ACKNOWLEDGMENTS

In addition to the formal credit lines accompanying illustrations, grateful acknowledgment is made for the permission to reprint the copyright material and warm thanks to the friends who lent and permitted the use of photographs taken by them or from their collections.

Grateful acknowledgment is also made of the help received during the preliminary search for photographs at The Margaret Herrick Library, Academy of Motion Picture Arts and Sciences; The American Film Institute Center for Advanced Film Studies; and The Museum of Modern Art Film Stills Archive.

Copyright © 1976 by Irene Sharaff
Library of Congress Catalog Card Number 75-43903
ISBN 0-442-27527-7

All rights reserved. No part of this work covered by the copyright
hereon may be reproduced or used in any form or by any
means — graphic, electronic, or mechanical, including photocopying,
recording, taping, or information storage and retrieval
systems — without written permission of the publisher.

The author and Van Nostrand Reinhold Company have taken all
possible care to trace the ownership of every work of art reproduced in
this book and to make full acknowledgment for its use. If any errors
have accidentally occurred, they will be corrected in subsequent
editions, provided notification is sent to the publisher.
Manufactured in the United States of America.

Designed by Loudan Enterprises

Published in 1976 by Van Nostrand Reinhold Company
A Division of Litton Educational Publishing, Inc.
450 West 33rd Street
New York, NY 10001

Van Nostrand Reinhold Limited
1410 Birchmount Road
Scarborough, Ontario M1P 2E7, Canada

Van Nostrand Reinhold Australia Pty. Ltd.
17 Queen Street
Mitcham, Victoria 3132, Australia

Van Nostrand Reinhold Company Ltd.
Molly Millars Lane
Wokingham, Berkshire, England

16 15 14 13 12 11 10 9 8 7 6 5 4 3 2 1

Library of Congress Cataloging in Publication Data
Sharaff, Irene.
  Broadway and Hollywood.
  Includes index.
  1. Sharaff, Irene. 2. Costume design. I. Title.
TT505.S5A33   746.9'2'0924 [B]   75-43903
ISBN 0-442-27527-7

Contents

        Costumes Designed by Irene Sharaff   6

1.   Apprenticeship   8

2.   A year abroad / Theater in Paris / Haute couture   15

3.   *Alice in Wonderland*   18

4.   Step to Broadway / "Easter Parade" / *On Your Toes*   26

5.   Mike Todd's revues / Mike and the King of Siam   36

6.   Placing costumes in period, place, character / Handling colors for stage and screen   43

7.   MGM in the forties / Adrian / *Meet Me in St. Louis* / Designing and shooting schedules / Changing role of designers   58

8.   Back and forth between Broadway and Hollywood   67

9.   *An American in Paris* / "Born in a Trunk"   72

10.   *The King and I*   78

11.   *Porgy and Bess* / *Can-Can* / Khrushchev visits 20th Century-Fox   93

12.   *West Side Story* / *Candide*   100

13.   *Cleopatra*   105

14.   Elizabeth / Stardom / Barbra   116

15.   *Justine* / *The Great White Hope*   124

        Index   134

COSTUMES DESIGNED BY IRENE SHARAFF

THEATER

1932	ALICE IN WONDERLAND (scenery & costumes; Donaldson Award)	Civic Repertory / Eva Le Gallienne
1933	AS THOUSANDS CHEER	Sam Harris
1934	LIFE BEGINS AT 8:40	Shubert
	THE GREAT WALTZ	Max Gordon
1935	CRIME AND PUNISHMENT (scenery & costumes)	Victor Wolfson
	PARADE	Theatre Guild
	JUBILEE	Sam Harris
	ROSMERSHOLM (scenery & costumes)	Shubert
1936	IDIOT'S DELIGHT	Theatre Guild
	ON YOUR TOES	Dwight Deere Wiman
	WHITE HORSE INN	Erik Charell
1937	VIRGINIA	Rockefeller City Center
	I'D RATHER BE RIGHT	Sam Harris
1938	BOYS FROM SYRACUSE	George Abbott
1939	THE AMERICAN WAY	Sam Harris & Max Gordon
	STREETS OF PARIS	Shubert
	GAY NEW ORLEANS	Michael Todd / World's Fair
1940	BOYS AND GIRLS TOGETHER	Ed Wynn
	ALL IN FUN	Leonard Sillman
1941	LADY IN THE DARK	Sam Harris
	THE LAND IS BRIGHT	Max Gordon
	SUNNY RIVER	Max Gordon
	BANJO EYES	Albert Lewis
1942	BY JUPITER	Dwight Deere Wiman
	STAR AND GARTER	Michael Todd
	COUNT ME IN	Shubert
1945	BILLION DOLLAR BABY	Oliver Smith & Paul Feigay
1946	THE WOULD-BE GENTLEMAN	Michael Todd
	G. I. HAMLET	Michael Todd
1948	BONANZA BOUND	Herman Levin, Smith, Feigay
	MAGDALENA	Homer Curran & Edwin Lester
1949	MONTSERRAT	Kermit Bloomgarden
1950	DANCE ME A SONG	Dwight Deere Wiman
	MIKE TODD'S PEEPSHOW	Michael Todd
1951	THE KING AND I (Antoinette Perry & Donaldson Awards)	Rodgers & Hammerstein
	A TREE GROWS IN BROOKLYN	George Abbott
1952	OF THEE I SING (revival)	
1953	ME AND JULIET	Rodgers & Hammerstein
	THE KING AND I (London production)	Rodgers & Hammerstein
1954	BY THE BEAUTIFUL SEA	Fryer & Carr
	ON YOUR TOES (revival)	George Abbott
1956	SHANGRI-LA	Fryer & Carr
	CANDIDE	Ethel Linder Reiner
	HAPPY HUNTING	Jo Mielziner
1957	SMALL WAR ON MURRAY HILL	Playwrights' Company
	WEST SIDE STORY	Griffith & Prince
1958	FLOWER DRUM SONG	Rodgers & Hammerstein
1959	JUNO	Playwrights' Company
1960	DO RE MI	David Merrick
1963	JENNY	Crawford, Halliday, Pakula
	THE GIRL WHO CAME TO SUPPER	Herman Levin
	BOYS FROM SYRACUSE (London production)	
1964	FUNNY GIRL	Ray Stark
	THE KING AND I (revival)	Lincoln Center
1965	SWEET CHARITY	Fryer, Carr, Harris
1967	HALLELUJAH, BABY!	Selden, James, Nussbaum, Rigby
1972	IRENE (costumes for Debbie Reynolds)	Selden, Rigby, Minskoff

MOTION PICTURES

1943	MADAME CURIE	Metro-Goldwyn-Mayer
1944	MEET ME IN ST. LOUIS	Metro-Goldwyn-Mayer
1945	YOLANDA AND THE THIEF	Metro-Goldwyn-Mayer
	ZIEGFELD FOLLIES (Traviata & Limehouse numbers)	Metro-Goldwyn-Mayer
1946	THE BEST YEARS OF OUR LIVES	Samuel Goldwyn
1947	THE SECRET LIFE OF WALTER MITTY	Samuel Goldwyn
	THE BISHOP'S WIFE	Samuel Goldwyn
1948	A SONG IS BORN	Samuel Goldwyn
	EVERY GIRL SHOULD BE MARRIED	R K O
1951	** AN AMERICAN IN PARIS (scenery & costumes for Ballet Sequence)	Metro-Goldwyn-Mayer
	HUCKLEBERRY FINN	Metro-Goldwyn-Mayer
1952	* CALL ME MADAM	20th Century-Fox
1953	* BRIGADOON	Metro-Goldwyn-Mayer
1954	* A STAR IS BORN (scenery & costumes for "Born In A Trunk")	Warner Bros.
1955	* GUYS AND DOLLS	Samuel Goldwyn
1956	** THE KING AND I	20th Century-Fox
1959	* PORGY AND BESS	Samuel Goldwyn
1960	* CAN-CAN	20th Century-Fox
1961	** WEST SIDE STORY	Mirisch Bros.
	* FLOWER DRUM SONG	Universal-International
1963	** CLEOPATRA (costumes for Elizabeth Taylor)	20th Century-Fox
1965	THE SANDPIPER	Metro-Goldwyn-Mayer
1966	** WHO'S AFRAID OF VIRGINIA WOOLF?	Warner Bros.
1967	* THE TAMING OF THE SHREW (costumes for Elizabeth Taylor)	Columbia Pictures
	FUNNY GIRL (costumes for Barbra Streisand)	Ray Stark / Columbia
1969	* HELLO, DOLLY!	20th Century-Fox
	JUSTINE	20th Century-Fox
1970	THE GREAT WHITE HOPE	20th Century-Fox
1976	THE OTHER SIDE OF MIDNIGHT	20th Century-Fox

* ACADEMY NOMINATION FOR AWARD
** OSCAR AWARD

BALLETS

1934	UNION PACIFIC	Ballet Russe de Monte Carlo
1937	JEU DE CARTES (scenery & costumes)	George Balanchine
1945	INTERPLAY	American Ballet Theatre
1946	FACSIMILE	American Ballet Theatre
1950	AGE OF ANXIETY	New York City Ballet
	DESIGN WITH STRINGS	American Ballet Theatre
1953	FANFARE (scenery & costumes)	New York City Ballet
1956	THE CONCERT	New York City Ballet
	RIB OF EVE	American Ballet Theatre
1958	THREE × THREE	Jerome Robbins Ballet: U.S.A.
1968	SLAUGHTER ON TENTH AVENUE	New York City Ballet
1971	PAMTGG	New York City Ballet
	PRINTEMPS	New York City Ballet
	THE CONCERT (revival)	New York City Ballet
1972	INTERPLAY (revival)	Joffrey Ballet
1975	THE CONCERT (London production)	The Royal Ballet, London
1976	FANFARE (scenery & costumes, new edition)	New York City Ballet

TELEVISION

1953	FORD ANNIVERSARY TELECAST (costumes for Mary Martin and Ethel Merman)
1958	DUPONT SHOW OF THE MONTH — ALADDIN

1. Apprenticeship

On a summer afternoon in 1928 — it now seems aeons ago — I waited outside The Civic Repertory Theatre to meet Aline Bernstein, the scenic and costume designer who had just become the art director. The meeting had been arranged by Eva Le Gallienne, an established star on Broadway, who founded the Civic because she believed that New York should have a repertory theater. She had seen a portfolio of my sketches, shown it to Aline and suggested that she might use me as her assistant in the coming season.

I was extremely nervous waiting for Aline. Still a student in art school, I had no experience in the theater, and my chances of getting a job were very slight. I had pictured Aline as formidable. However, suddenly the doors of the theater lobby opened and she walked towards me; middle-aged, short, roly-poly, with large hazel eyes and a warm smile, she was entrancing. She wore a simple black suit, white shirtwaist, and to my delight, on her low-heeled slippers a pair of eighteenth-century American buckles.

She asked me innumerable questions. In spite of my fear that she would consider me too young and inexperienced for the job, she finally said that my sketches showed a great deal of talent and that she would take me on as her assistant — though it is perhaps more accurate to say "apprentice," because for the first six months I received no salary. It was nevertheless the start of three years of intensive training in the theater, invaluable, and perhaps possible only in repertory theater.

At the end of that interview, Aline handed me three scripts of the new productions in the repertory for the coming season and told me to make costume and prop lists for each of them. She added that since I knew how to draft blueprints for scenery, she would sometimes expect me to do that too, along with other chores. I was to report for work on the first of September. As I walked away from that brief meeting, I knew that I was about to enter a world about which I knew very little but one that I longed to become part of.

Eva Le Gallienne.

Aline Bernstein. Courtesy Edla Bernstein Cusick.

The Civic was on Fourteenth Street between Sixth and Seventh Avenues. Built in 1866, it had changed hands and names several times, until in 1879 it became famous as The Fourteenth Street Theatre, the home of melodrama. When the theater district moved uptown, the Victorian house suffered neglect, and a third-rate Italian opera company occupied it for a time. In 1926 Le Gallienne took it over for her repertory theater. The stage was well proportioned, and although the auditorium was shabby, it was spacious and comfortable and looked very much like the Old Vic in London. From 1926 to 1932 Le Gallienne presented there thirty-four productions — a record in theater in New York.

When I reported for work at the Civic, I had carefully done my homework. I had made lists of the costumes and props for the three scripts, and in my anxiety not to miss anything I memorized all three plays. When I saw Aline, she had a large stack of costume sketches to be put into work and a complete set of blueprints for the scenery. From the first day that I worked with her, Aline treated me as a colleague, showed no annoyance at my lack of expertise, and was understanding when I made mistakes.

It was part of my job to look for samples of different materials that Aline needed for her costume designs. After she had chosen from the bundles of swatches, I would then go and buy the required yardage.

The Civic Repertory Theatre. Courtesy Eva Le Gallienne.

I had also to find the necessary props for each new production. When they were unobtainable or too expensive, I was asked to make them. My first assignment was to find appropriate china and cutlery for Molière's *Le Bourgeois Gentilhomme*, which was the new play that opened the Civic season that year. I discovered the restaurant supply shops on the Bowery and selected bowls and plates along with some discontinued patterns of cutlery. Glue, papier-mâché, and gold leaf applied with great care, and hopefully with taste, made them look convincingly enough like seventeenth-century table settings. As a guide, I used a French history book for children, which was illustrated with simple drawings of ordinary things used daily in different periods. For this production I was also asked to paint a portrait of Monsieur Jourdain on a canvas six feet by four, which was to look like one of those extravagant pictures painted in the time of Louis XIV. It never occurred to me that I could not do it or that it was a tough assignment for an apprentice. Today I would certainly think twice before tackling such a task.

New York is a mecca for an extraordinary variety of exotic merchandise from all over the world. For me, at the Civic, New York was a vast hunting ground in some corner of which I would find the things needed in the various plays, usually in small shops away from the mainstream of stores. Bolts of inexpensive materials of little use to the average shopper were useful for adding an extra touch of theatricality to costumes: printed cottons from Portugal, probably originally shipped over for cheap curtain fabrics, made wonderful pantaloons for some of the pirates in *Peter Pan*; thin silk gauze from the Philippines, woven for lampshades and buried in the basement of a store on Hester Street, made a lovely peignoir; cheap linen from Ireland was turned into peasant blouses for a Chekhov play.

In looking for a small hand-machine for rolling cigarettes, an important prop for a Spanish play, I discovered a whole section of tobacco shops downtown near the East River, and in one of them, tucked away on a shelf, I found the little machine no longer in demand in New York though still in use in some parts of Spain.

Having worked at the Neighborhood Playhouse on Grand Street, Aline knew well the little shops on the Lower East Side and would occasionally go with me. And it was at Hammacher Schlemmer, at that time a large hardware store off Lafayette Street, that we one day bought brass toilet chains — such as one pulled on the old-style w.c. — by the yard to turn into Renaissance necklaces for Tybalt and others in *Romeo and Juliet*.

It was in *Romeo and Juliet*, when more extras were needed, that I had to join in the stately dance at the Capulet ball, dressed in a gorgeous mustard velveteen gown. In the same production, muffled in a hooded cape I was a mourner alongside Burgess Meredith, who was also an apprentice filling in as an extra in the Tomb Scene. It happened one evening that Paris, in the interval between his two appearances in that scene, had thought to finish a hand of poker with some stagehands, and missed his cue for the second entrance. On stage we waited. In the dreadful pause suddenly Agnes MacCarthy, another mourner under a cape, called out desperately "The Prince is coming! The Prince is COMING!" Paris dashed most unmournfully on to the stage. As we filed off the stage afterwards, Agnes apologized in consternation to everyone around. I can still hear her shrill voice: "Oh I *am* sorry. I'm terribly sorry. One doesn't ad lib in Shakespeare!"

For period plays at the Civic of course we visited secondhand-furniture and junk shops. We picked up some good turn-of-the-century pieces for the plays with Victorian settings. Fortunately, when elegant French furniture was needed, one of the backers lent some of her signed pieces, which had to be returned to her apartment after each performance.

Alla Nazimova returned to the theater after some years in Hollywood to play the part of Madame Ranevsky in the Civic's production of Chekhov's *The Cherry Orchard*. She had earlier made a tremendous hit on Broadway as Nora in Ibsen's *The Doll's House*, but had then gone to California. New and younger audiences, including myself, had never seen her on the stage. *The Cherry Orchard* was the second new production of the season when I started at the Civic. Because several plays were being rehearsed, the schedule was very tight, and Nazimova and the cast had to rehearse at night. I did not have time to watch any of the plays being rehearsed during the day, so that the Chekhov play, rehearsing at night, was my introduction to how the direction and rehearsals of a play developed. Since then, I have watched many re-

Alla Nazimova as Madame Ranevsky in *The Cherry Orchard*. Photograph by Vandamm. Theater Collection, The New York Public Library at Lincoln Center. Astor, Lenox and Tilden Foundations.

hearsals more exciting, better directed, with distinguished casts, but none has had for me the magic of Nazimova's *Cherry Orchard*.

The play was set at the turn of the century, and Aline had found some original Worth dresses for Nazimova. They were not only exquisite but were in perfect condition. All were either black or cream in color, and the person for whom these clothes had originally been made must have had a figure almost identical with Nazimova's, for very few alterations were needed. Among them, a black dinner gown of handmade silk lace over a foundation of chiffon and taffeta was typical of Worth's genius. It would now be a priceless possession in any costume museum.

Nazimova was in her middle fifties when she played Madame Ranevsky. Although her features were large and rather coarse, across the footlights she projected the image of a strikingly handsome woman. Her slightly pockmarked face had an ivory tinge, which she exaggerated by using a startlingly white make-up.

After *The Cherry Orchard* opened, I often sat in Nazimova's dressing room to watch her put on her make-up. This theatrical art, which is part of every actor's bag of tricks, is a ritual that all performers enjoy, but as Nazimova was a good amateur painter, her approach to applying make-up differed from that of other performers I have watched. Various shades of color were carefully blended over her high cheekbones; then, when she placed a dab of white on the bridge of her nose, which was rather thick and which always reminded me of the dilated nostrils of a frightened horse, it suddenly appeared aquiline and aristocratic. It took her over an hour to create this new face. The final touch was always a flourish of a large swan's-down puff laden with fine rice powder, which sent a cloud of white dust through the air around her. On the strip of thin gauze that she had wrapped around her head she would pin and firmly anchor her period wig. When the ritual of making up was completed, she would drop her black silk kimono, step into her costume laid out on the floor, struggle to hook it up the back, and then slowly step back to survey herself in the long mirror. The transformation never ceased to be startling, for she looked like a Boldini portrait come to life.

The first year of working with Aline went quickly, and when the season was over she asked me to spend part of the summer helping her draft the blueprints for the scenery that she had to design for the next season. Under the drafting table at which I worked was a bushel basket in which Aline stored the bulky manuscript of Thomas Wolfe's *Look Homeward, Angel*. She had been influential in getting the book published and behaved very possessively about it. Both Aline and Tom eventually wrote about their romance. At the time at the Civic, however, Le Gallienne's interest was in Tom's great height, and she kept asking him to play one of the pirates in *Peter Pan*. For me, the important point was that when I could not find Aline at the theater, I was able to reach her at Tom's studio around the corner.

In her own studio Aline had a large library of costume and theater décor. These books became the springboard to my fascination with the long and complex history of clothes. As a student, studying period and ethnic clothes was at first merely delight to the eyes, but when I began to reflect about the reasons why silhouettes and styles in fashion constantly change, I began to look at clothes in the past and the present in a completely different way. They not only represent an important aspect of social history but also deep and curious psychological needs of human beings to decorate themselves.

I worked with Aline for about three years and in that time helped her on about fifteen plays. When, after the second year, she started to design for Broadway productions, I was responsible for the execution of some of her designs for the Civic. The stock market crash hit the Civic as badly as everything else. Le Gallienne decided to close the theater for a year with the hope that eventually she could raise funds to reopen. I had enough savings for a round-trip ticket to Europe and found that by careful planning I could spend the next year in Paris.

2. A year abroad / Theater in Paris / Haute couture

I arrived in Paris on a memorably beautiful day in July, 1931. Even for the sophisticated, Paris in the thirties was an extraordinarily exciting city. I had spent all my life in New York and had been no farther afield than Boston, Philadelphia, and Fort Wayne, Indiana. Therefore Paris seemed like a glorious birthday almost every day. I discovered Paris by walking through its streets and parks and market places; like most tourists, I visited its museums, churches, and art galleries. When I gradually began to know my way around the city, and when I realized that I had a whole year, I no longer felt I had to see everything at once.

No one could have lived in Paris at that time without being aware of the political climate that each day became more disturbing. I was made more conscious of it one afternoon at an American friend's house where Putzi Hanfstaengl, a member of Hitler's inner circle, mesmerized the guests by his piano playing and a hysterical extolment of Der Fuehrer.

The world of the Paris theater and of the Cirques d'Hiver and Medrano made Broadway and the Civic seem old-fashioned. Most of the plays in the commercial theater seemed much better than those in New York. The experimental theaters, the Comédie Française, and the Odéon were more exciting than any theater I had ever seen. The theater designing in its handling of color and striking simplicity was stunning. Christian Bérard, Pavel Tchelitchev, and André Derain were just three of the painters designing in the theater in Paris that year. I found their work overwhelming. One of the most beautifully designed productions I have ever seen was Alexandre Benois' presentation of *La Dame Aux Camélias* with Ida Rubenstein as Marguerite Gautier.

One visit in Paris influenced me from then on in using white whenever possible. For I spent an enchanting afternoon with Brancusi in his large studio off the Rue Vaugirard and was dazzled by the large white room, the white pieces of sculpture, and Brancusi himself in white coveralls and a white hat. He was working on a large white marble seal, now in The Museum of Modern Art in New York. There was a fine layer of marble dust over everything in the studio and moving around it was like walking on granulated sugar.

My first look at the world of high fashion was at a collection designed by Elsa Schiaparelli. Her name is now legendary, associated with her dynamic creations and with Shocking Pink.

High fashion has always been served by many designers with varying talents, but the designers who have changed attitudes towards clothes and created new forms of dress have been very few. Significantly, between the two World Wars, the designers who invented new attitudes towards women's clothes and finally eliminated the last traces of the nineteenth century were six women. While Poiret, before the First World War and into the first part of the twenties, pioneered the straight line and banished the corset, the six designers who really took the first bold stride into the twentieth century were the three Callot sisters, Vionnet, Chanel, and Schiaparelli.

One looks at what these designers accomplished with a twinge of nostalgia, for they made their métier an art and displayed a certain splendor and great style. Elegance of true simplicity characterized most of the designs of Callot and of Vionnet — in the quality of the fabrics they used, the high standards of workmanship in the cut and construction of their clothes, the ingenious use of beads, tassels, embroidery, and their sophisticated palettes. One thinks of the delicate hues Callot used under the influence of chinoiserie, and the black, beige, brown, and rose-pink associated with Vionnet. The Callot salon introduced lounging pajamas, lace dresses, the dipping and the scalloped hemlines. And Vionnet invented the bias cut for the complete dress, with the cowl neck on some models, which did so much for the fit and hang of clothes.

The foundation of present fashion might be said, however, to have been laid by Gabrielle Chanel. With one sweep of her shears Chanel not only cut women's skirts to the knees but also shortened their hair. She got down to basics and designed clothes that were functional: the wool jersey dress, the suit, the plain white shirt, cardigans, the loose skirt with slit pockets at the sides. With these she used berets and small hats and lots of costume jewelry, particularly strings of fake pearls. More than anyone, Chanel gave women a new feeling of physical freedom which changed their attitudes about themselves.

About ten years after Chanel made sweeping changes in the concept of women's clothes, Elsa Schiaparelli succeeded her as the most innovative designer in the thirties. Although Africa, the Middle East, and Asia had to a certain extent influenced fashion in the past, Schiaparelli used their ethnic clothes as the basis of many of her designs. With very little change a North African burnoose became a cape worn over a simple evening dress; a maharajah's coat turned into an afternoon tunic. The padded jacket worn for centuries in China was copied down to its ingeniously tied buttons. Besides these ageless garments, modern and smart in Schiaparelli's adaptations, some of her designs were based on the eminently practical clothes worn by French workers. The surrealist movement also influenced her designs. Her audacious imagination adapted all kinds of objects and motifs into decoration and accessories for her clothes. The smart little black dress she made famous was perfect for these additional touches, and she was the first to use the zipper. Although she used black for day and evening, one remembers her designs also for their use of vivid colors, such as scarlet, purple, and her own Shocking Pink.

3. *Alice in Wonderland*

I had been in Paris about five months when Eva Le Gallienne arrived for a visit. She had managed to find backing to re-open the Civic. At lunch she told me about the plays in the repertory and the new productions she planned for the season of 1932. In speaking of a production of *Alice in Wonderland* with music by a young English composer, Richard Addinsell, she said, "I think it would be a good idea if you designed the scenery and costumes for it." I did not quite believe what I heard and put it down to the flow of wine at lunch. When the script came the next day, I realized that she had been serious. When I read the script, I saw that she had worked out the physical scheme of the play and that my job would be to re-create the scenery and costumes as drawn by Tenniel within the framework of her plan.

I bought a copy of the book with the Tenniel illustrations and looked with renewed interest at the role that his drawings play in the telling of the story. To design the production for the Civic — which occupied most of the rest of my stay in Paris — a shift of focus was necessary to translate scenery and costumes according to Tenniel to the three-dimensional stage and to adjust the proportions of the whole and each part and detail. To convey the Tenniel texture closely associated in the memories of most of us with *Alice*, I used white sailcloth as the basic fabric for both the scenery and the costumes, drawing on it brushstrokes similar in form and application to the fine cross-hatched pen lines of Tenniel's technique (though proportionately broader, of course, to carry the effect across the footlights). I copied his form of chiaroscuro, giving the backgrounds and costumes their own painted shadows even though the stage lighting would produce certain highlights and shadows.

The design of the scenery had the background and setting drawn on a huge scroll like a typewriter ribbon, fed scene by scene from a spool on the left across the back of the stage to a spool on the right. Small pieces of constructed scenery needed in some scenes moved on two small flat wagons on sunken tracks across the stage. All scene changes thus took place in the sight of the audience.

The sketches for the costumes had to take into account changes of proportion and, above all, that the clothes had to be functional. They were going to be worn and take the kind of beating that costumes in the theater must endure, and they had not only to fit and look well but allow the actors freedom of movement. I made the sketches like architectural drawings and drew the figures under the superimposed Tenniel characters, working out, for instance, how many inches away from the body the tiered skirt of the White Queen had to be and the size of the padding for the tummies of Tweedledee and Tweedledum. The costumes of the animals became complicated, and Tenniel had to be altered to enable the actors to move in the costumes. Most of the characters moreover needed full masks; these had to be in proportion with the rest of the costumes, yet the actors had to see out of the masks.

Section of the scenery roll.

Tenniel's Ugly Duchess.

"A Grotesque Woman" by Massys (1465–1530), which sparked or certainly added to the Tenniel Ugly Duchess. Reproduced by courtesy of the Trustees, The National Gallery, London.

Costume sketch for the Ugly Duchess.

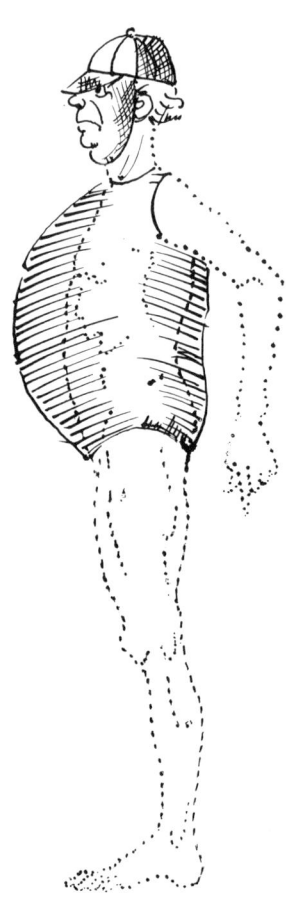

Tweedledee with padding and mask.

Tweedledee dressed.

The Mad Hatter.

The entire production was designed in black and white except for Alice's blue dress, the red Victorian chair made oversize so that Alice looked very small, and the crimson of the Red Queen's robe. The most important lesson I learned in making these sketches had to do with sharpening the sense of proportion, which is surely vital in all designing.

While preparing the production of *Alice in Wonderland*, and before it went into rehearsal, I worked as Aline's assistant on the three other new productions. For me the most memorable part of these plays was watching Ethel Barrymore rehearse the role of the Duchess of Parma in *L'Aiglon* and listening to her many amusing stories about the theater and about making films in Hollywood.

Pepe Schildkraut and his wife took me to Coney Island one evening because he wanted to get some hand-props for his role of Liliom in that play, which opened the season. As we walked on the Boardwalk, I spotted a stunted pig on a leash in one of the sideshows. A squealing piglet was needed for the Ugly Duchess, when her baby turned into one, and I was sure that the owner of this Coney Island pig could tell me where to get one. He insisted on first showing off his fat little pig performing some simple tricks before telling the name of a farm, adding in deepest confidence that a piglet, fed gin, would not grow. I soon discovered, however, after getting a baby pig, that it took like a toper to gin and moreover grew enormous. During the run of the play four little pigs in succession replaced the first one.

In putting the production of *Alice*, which was a singularly large one, into work, there was no time to think about it being my first complete production or about the rather momentous step from being Aline's assistant to having one of my own, an apprentice from the Civic's acting school. Cleon Throckmorton's scenic studio began work on the construction of the scenery, and the Civic's head carpenter helped me with some of the mechanical problems which I could not handle. The roll of sailcloth for the scenery was mounted on the wooden spools and stretched across the back of the stage. Every night, after the current performance, a crew of scenic painters and I painted the Tenniel drawings that I had enlarged on the white background of the roll. I snatched a few hours sleep on a rolled up velvet curtain which was stored in one of the boxes in the lower tier of the auditorium and in the morning attended the fittings of the costumes. When these were ready, they were brought down on dummies to the stage, and I painted them while keeping an eye on the progress of the scenery.

Remo Bufano, a funny little man, a well-known sculptor and puppeteer, modeled the Carpenter, the Walrus, and the oysters into large marionettes; after they were articulated, costumes were made for them and then painted as on the other costumes. Remo also executed the masks and some of the props, such as the flamingos wielded as mallets in the famous croquet game.

Since the first dress rehearsal of any play is an unavoidable agony in the theater, a few recollections might give some idea of that kind of nightmare. Bringing together all of the elements that form the physical aspect of a production into a fairly coherent whole is much like coping with a huge, unwieldy jigsaw puzzle. Stagehands confront scenery that they see for the first time. Electrical equipment has to be sorted out and placed. In a very short period all has to be in order and functioning properly. The company trail on to the stage in their costumes also for the first time, usually holding parts of the costumes in their hands. The director watching all of this is generally the first to become impatient over how slowly everything is being put together, and makes quick judgments and decisions about details before the production can be seen as a whole and in running order.

Responsible for everything visible on the stage, I experienced for the first time that sickening feeling which accompanies the exposure of one's work in the theater. For a moment I wished I had done it differently. As happens almost invariably and perhaps inevitably as a release from tensions, someone loses his temper. In this instance Le Gallienne's wrath exploded at me when a table collapsed. This table had had to be constructed to extend larger and fold smaller according to the peculiar demands of the story. The head carpenter and I had spent hours with the mechanic who made this vital prop, testing that it would work properly, but apparently en route to the theater part of the delicate mechanism had snapped.

Although *Alice in Wonderland* was enormously successful, its run alone could not carry the repertory or save the economic situation of the Civic. When the Civic closed, I was out of a job and did not have the slightest idea how to go about getting another.

4. Step to Broadway/"Easter Parade"/ On Your Toes

Luckily, almost immediately after the Civic closed, I received a telephone call from Irving Berlin's secretary setting an interview for the next day. When I arrived at the Music Box Theatre, I was shown to the penthouse where Irving Berlin had his office. There I found him in shirt sleeves, chewing gum vehemently in time with his fingers on the keyboard. He said that he had been trying to locate me for weeks and had finally gotten my telephone number from Moss Hart. He then explained that Moss had written a revue, *As Thousands Cheer*, for which he was writing the music and lyrics. Hassard Short would direct the show; having seen photographs in London papers of my work in *Alice in Wonderland*, he had cabled Berlin to find me to design the costumes in one number in the revue. Berlin asked me if I was interested. Needless to say I was agog and could hardly contain myself when he made an appointment for me to meet Hassard Short. Thus I started on Broadway.

Hassard's office was in a dressing room on the second floor of the theater. He did not have a secretary and the door to the room was open when I arrived. He apparently did not hear my knock. As I stood in the doorway our eyes met in the mirror in front of which he was trying on a gold mesh necklace and obviously admiring the reflection. He looked at me rather sheepishly, quickly removed the necklace, and then asked me to come in.

Hassard was an English director who had started in the theater as an actor. He looked like a clergyman. Years later he told me that his father had been a well-known churchman. Constantly looking for new talent, Hassard gave many young and inexperienced people their first chance to work on Broadway. I was very lucky to have been one of them. At that first meeting we immediately sat at his desk, which was cluttered with scripts, photographs, and scenic sketches, and he explained the general idea of the revue and the number he wanted me to design.

The format of the revue was based on that of a newspaper, the various sections being presented in satirical skits and musical numbers all of which amounted to comments on the current scene. One large production number was to be based on a comic strip popular at the time. He explained that he liked what he had seen of my work in *Alice* and suggested the same technique for the comic strip characters.

As we talked about the number he suddenly asked if I had ever designed period costumes. I explained that I had made many sketches for different period plays, but that *Alice* had been my first job as a theater designer. He mentioned another number in the revue that I might design but cautiously suggested that I first make a few sketches for him to see.

The number he had in mind was the "Easter Parade," taking its cue from the rotogravure section of *The New York Times* Sunday edition. How many people, I wonder, remember those few sheets of photographs printed in sepia ink which used to be a distinctive feature of the Sunday newspaper? Setting the period for the number back to 1885, I designed the costumes in a wide range of browns from the lightest to the darkest, and from the warm tones to the cold, strategically using touches of cool and warm whites among the bitter chocolate brown, umbers, siennas, and taupes. By using a wide range of fabrics for variety in texture, the final effect managed to translate the glossy sepia pages into theatrical terms.

It was not till Hassard Short had seen the sketches that he gave me the job to design the costumes for the comic-strip number and "Easter Parade." And not until I had designed both numbers that I had my first taste of the problems and pressures of having costumes made for the Broadway theater. Eaves Costume Company executed the costumes, so for the first time I worked with that costume house run by the Geoly family.

One morning when I was going to see Hassard, I stopped at the drugstore next to the Music Box Theatre for coffee and found Moss Hart at the counter having breakfast. I had met Moss at Aline's parties and remembered only his proclivity for wisecracks and gold trinkets. At the drugstore counter that morning his insecurity over the revue was unmistakable. He was frightened that the show might fail, saying over and over again that if it was a flop, he would have to go back to live in the Bronx. Happily, Moss's fears were soon put to rest, for *As Thousands Cheer* was a tremendous hit. When I worked with him again, however, I was surprised to hear the same cry all over again.

After my first venture on Broadway under Hassard Short's wing, I worked on production numbers in several musicals and also designed Leonid Massine's ballet *Union Pacific*. I remember *On Your Toes* in 1936 in clearer detail perhaps because it was my first opportunity to design the costumes for an entire Broadway musical. More important, it had a score by Richard Rodgers and lyrics by Lorenz Hart, was directed by George Abbott, and is something of a landmark in the American musical theater because it introduced ballet as an integral part of the story and the production.

A lady. "Easter Parade" number in *As Thousands Cheer*.

A girl. "Easter Parade."   A gent. "Easter Parade."

George Balanchine, a genius of dance, was the choreographer. Tamara Geva and Ray Bolger were the stars. As established dancers — the one as a prima ballerina, the other as a top tap dancer — they were of course vital to the show and gave professional class to the production and particularly to the two prominent ballets. Besides "Slaughter on Tenth Avenue," which was integral to the story, there was another ballet, a take-off of *Scheherazade*, which posed an initial problem for the scenic designer, Jo Mielziner, and for me. Leon Bakst's pseudo-oriental designs for *Scheherazade* had been copied widely, influencing even the décor of movie houses, so Jo and I agreed to set the ballet in the late eighteenth century with, of course, a strong Persian accent. The wit required for the ballet to be a take-off — perilous situation, to say the least — depended on the impact of this combination on the contemporary eye.

The male dancers had Persian jackets with the inevitable tights. The girl dancers wore short tutus, transparent pantaloons, and bodices cut like Persian jackets. All the costumes were in colors derived from Persian miniatures. For the eighteenth-century element, stylized wigs were worn. With these, the girls also had large white hats, like immense poufs of whipped cream, such as the Incroyables in France affected at that time. Historically, the wigs and hats caricatured their own period.

As the curtain rose on the ballet on the opening night in Boston, the corps de ballet, in couples, danced slowly across the stage. There was a small but audible giggle in the theater. As the large hats bobbed up and down as though they too were dancing to the music, the audience broke into gales of laughter. When Tamara Geva made her entrance, legs wrapped around her partner, she thought the audience was laughing at her and immediately started to camp her dance, at first tentatively, then when the laughter engulfed the auditorium, with mad abandon. The company followed her lead and the whole thing became like a version of *Hellzapoppin'*. Uproarious, but hardly witty.

Rodgers, Hart, Balanchine, Abbott, and I were standing in the back of the house and were all, I think, stunned by what was happening on the stage. Balanchine paled visibly even in the dimmed light. At the end of the ballet the audience was in a state of exhaustion from laughing but broke into wild applause. With an absolutely straight face, Balanchine turned to us around him and declared that that was exactly how he from the start had wanted the ballet danced.

Girl dancer. *Scheherazade* take-off.

Boy dancer. *Scheherazade* take-off.

In the other and main ballet, "Slaughter on Tenth Avenue," Balanchine combined ballet and tap dancing. With equal skill Rodgers' music accommodated both forms of dance. The libretto allowed Tamara to dance in the technique of classical ballet, while Ray Bolger counterpointed with tap dancing. The set was a dingy waterfront bar with the corps de ballet dancing the roles of molls, pimps, and police, while Tamara was a striptease artist and Ray a professor of music.

In designing the girls' costumes I reduced them to the minimum. Long stockings hitched up by garters, tutus the shortest possible, low-cut bodices patterned on Victorian corsets, tiny amusing hats. The male dancers wore over-all tights with short tight jackets slashed with different colors. The general palette was in shades of sienna, dusty pink, and tones of indigo and violet. Tamara's and Ray's costumes in black and white made a sharp contrast.

Tamara's costume was actually double: under the striptease outfit which she shed on stage she had on a simple black bodice with a miniscule black tutu trimmed with fine white edging. When I was drawing the black costume, I did not like the way I had painted the tights; I did the sketch again, but instead of a light wash over the legs I painted the tights to look as though they were made of a coarse black mesh. I had not come across any tights manufactured like these. When the costumes were being made, I asked Jessie Zimmer who supplied hose and tights for theater productions to look for elastic net material. Elastic fabrics were then just starting to be manufactured and within a few days she found some elasticized net which was made into the tights. Stocking manufacturers soon noted these mesh tights as a new idea and began producing them fast for the mass market. Later, Paris in turn copied this idea for stockings.

Since *On Your Toes* almost every musical has included a ballet of one kind or another — in some instances even when there was no reason for a ballet. Certainly, since that show, dance numbers in a production have become more closely integrated with the show, and dancing has often been used to carry scenes or as a transition from one scene to another. With the aim more apparent each season to speed up the pace of shows, dance numbers and most solos and duos have grown more frenetic, indeed have reached the point of making other scenes in the show seem sluggishly slow.

Tamara Geva. "Slaughter on Tenth Avenue" ballet in *On Your Toes*.

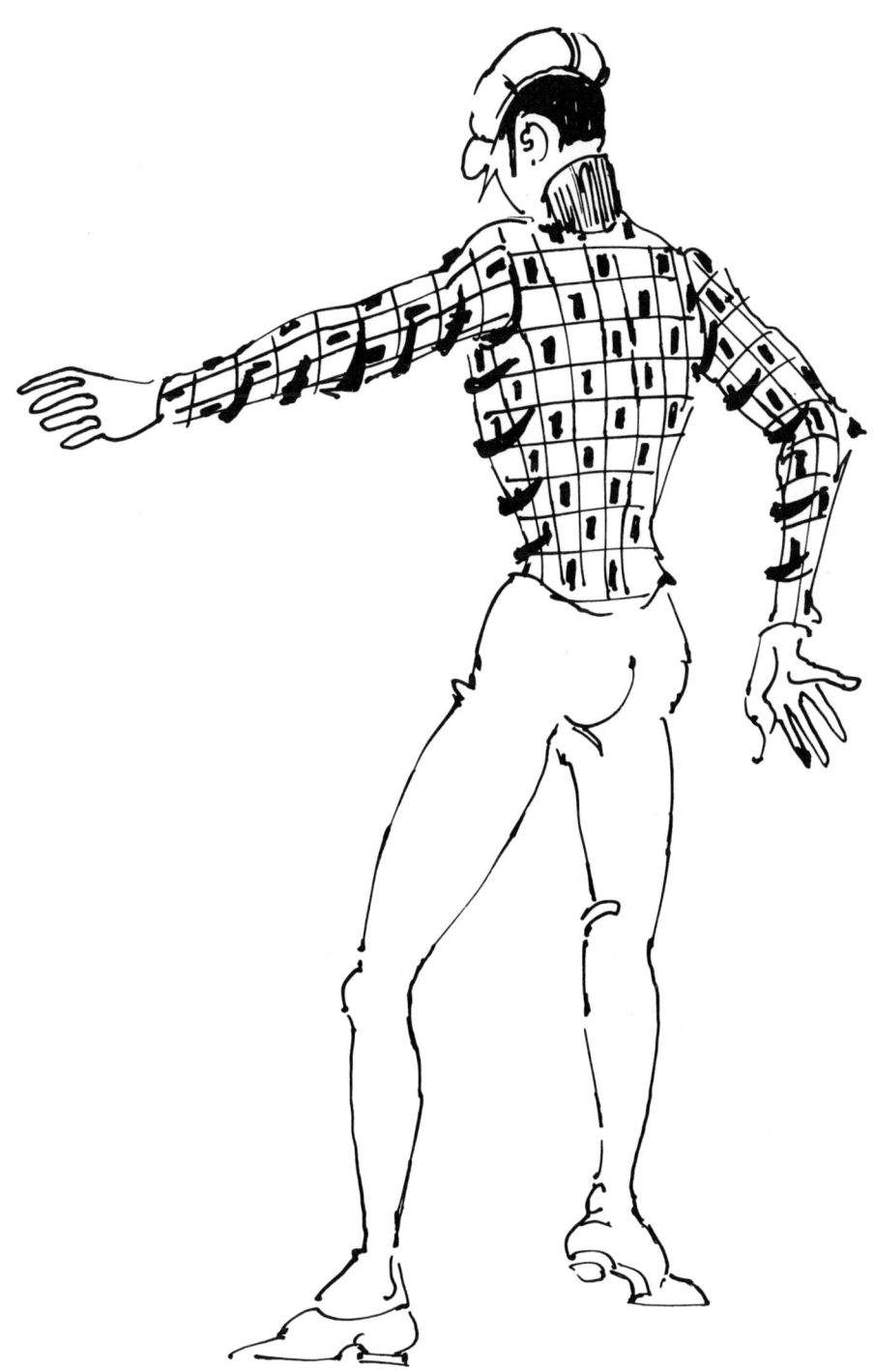

Ray Bolger. "Slaughter on Tenth Avenue" ballet in *On Your Toes*.

5. Mike Todd's revues/ Mike and the King of Siam

The revue on Broadway is now obsolete. Nightclub acts, TV spectacles, and the pretentious productions of Las Vegas hotels have replaced that form of theater for the general public. At its best, a revue was sophisticated entertainment. In 1942 and 1950 I designed costumes for two of the last successful revues on Broadway, both produced by Mike Todd.

Star and Garter was updated burlesque. For me it was one of the few shows, until then, which was mostly fun to work on. Hassard Short, who directed, turned old-fashioned burlesque to good effect. Gypsy Rose Lee, Bobby Clark, and Georgia Sothern used their own material, which for years they had been performing in burlesque houses across America. In the ambiance of a polished production their acts seemed as fresh as if they had just been invented.

At the beginning of her striptease number Georgia Sothern in a demure white chiffon ball gown looked like a blowsy Princess Margaret. When the music suddenly blared into "Hold that Tiger!" parts of her costume flew, on cue, piece by piece, in all directions. The costume presented problems: an ostensibly simple gown had also to be a tricky breakaway construction, and the paraphernalia underneath the gown had to be worked out in such detail that one was reminded of a watchmaker putting together the insides of a fine watch. The simple ball gown had also to hide another indispensable part of the costume. For before she stripped to the minimum G-string, she flung off a transparent petticoat, leaving in front a free-swinging panel weighted with tiny pieces of lead which she undulated to the beat of the music. Each part of this curious outfit had to be able to be detached with a flick of a finger nail. It took over five fittings to fix the mechanics of the costume for Georgia.

Gypsy's number did not whip the audience into a frenzy, for as a performer Gypsy's forte was a languid, fastidious style. She appeared as a chaste romantic girl in a long full skirt, white blouse, and a large leghorn hat.

As she sang her song, a natural lisp added to the effect. She then proceeded to peel off her clothes, dropping each piece daintily and pausing in time with the music. She shed several crisply starched petticoats and finally stood in a small G-string made of flowers crocheted in wool of pastel colors, with an extra flower on the tip of each breast. The general impression reminded one of those coy white marble statues fashionable at the turn of the century. She had invented a trick of pasting the crocheted flowers on her nipples in such a way that the tightly wound stem of each flower untwirled at a light tap of a finger. This gave a fillip to her curtain call and of course the audience applauded wildly.

The number I enjoyed most designing in the show was for the song "The Girl on *The Police Gazette*" by Irving Berlin, sung by a boy in his Sunday navy blue suit, with knickerbockers and starched collar, which struck a note of sentimental feeling reminiscent of "Easter Parade." *The Police Gazette* used to be considered risqué. Its trademark was the pink paper it was printed on. The entire number was therefore designed in pink and black, and as a revival of Victorian décor had just become popular, I based the designs for the costumes on those worn by "beefeaters" — not the yeomen of the guard but those sumptuous ladies in *The Black Crook*, one of the first American musicals.

What struck me as funny in the costumes of this show was matter of dead seriousness to the performers. Like the audiences, I was amused by the particular droop of the comedian's baggy pants, the fit of the short tight coat on the fall guy, the infinite variety of G-strings and bras. But to these veterans of burlesque every detail of what they wore, as with every gesture and move they made, had been worked out thoughtfully and achieved by long trial and error.

In *Peepshow*, Mike Todd's revue in 1950, I had to design for a second time a costume for a singer with a unique talent. She had appeared in a revue Mike had produced at the 1939 World's Fair, for which I had designed costumes for three numbers. Thus I had already coped once with the peculiar requirements of this performer's costume. Carrie Finnell was plump, with bleached hair, button nose, rosebud mouth, and a set stare through two humorless, watery blue eyes. She had spent many years developing the muscles of her melon-shaped breasts and had gained such a degree of muscular control that she was able to make each breast gyrate separately and alternately in time with the music. As the orchestra reached the end of the number with *tiddly-om-pom POM POM!* — the last two beats with clashing cymbals — one breast in split-second timing shot out from her bodice and back in, followed smartly by the thrust out and in of the other. She performed this extraordinary feat while singing an ordinary song in an ordinary voice out of her rosebud mouth. The audience howled. Women screamed hysterically, alarmed, and in sheer astonishment.

The first time I had to do a costume for Carrie Finnell, we met in a dressing room, one wall of which was a three-paneled mirror. She was wearing a short pink combination and looked like a kewpie doll. Asked about the requirements for the top of her dress, she showed me one of her own in baby-pink satin. I suggested another color but she brushed aside such a thought, saying that she always wore pink because it brought her good luck.

In examining the sample dress for the construction of the top, I asked her to show me how she did her special trick. "That, my dear, is none of your business," she replied firmly. But as I turned to leave, my eye caught her reflection in one of the mirrors, and out from the upper part of her combination popped one of her pink-tipped bosoms and just as swiftly popped back, like a naughty child sticking out her tongue at me.

Peepshow in itself was just one more production on Broadway but happened to lead to some situations unusual even for Broadway. For officials of Thailand were very unhappy over *The King and I* when that show opened in the next season. They probably did not know that, quite apart from and before *The King and I*, their young king helped set off Broadway's interest in Siam — as it was then still generally called. His debut as a composer in a New York production roughly coincided with the popularity of a reprint of *The English Governess at the Siamese Court* by Anna Leonowens, originally published in 1870, containing reminiscences of King Mongkut and his court around 1864. This book was the basis of the movie *Anna and the King of Siam* and of the musical *The King and I*. The collaboration between King Phumipon Aduldet and Mike Todd started during the preparatory stage of *Peepshow*.

Probably no one had more fun producing entertainment in one form or another than Mike Todd. He himself was a kind of entertainment. Cigar in mouth, he projected the image of a gambler or a gangster and fully enjoyed behaving in character. Certainly he was as tough as they come — ruthless, rough, sharp. But with his own brand of Jewish blarney and bluster managed to be likable, at times even charming. He was an entrepreneur with imagination, and he had eye and nerve — plenty of nerve. One instance might be given of how the wheels seemed to go round inside his head. For Mike was perhaps at his most ingenious when his financial backing was running dry. While *Peepshow* was in rehearsal and still being prepared for production, the backing indeed proved insufficient. To save the cost of elaborate scenery and costumes for the finale, Mike asked that the girls wear plain nude leotards. According to an idea he had just borne, the girls would be cavorting in a huge bubble bath.

At the dress rehearsal the finale did not start till 2:00 A.M. An enormous canvas tank was wheeled downstage, taking up the whole stage of the Winter Garden Theatre. In the empty auditorium Mike sat patiently waiting to see how his brainchild would look. The rest of us were exhausted but still curious. At this critical moment, the prop man came out from the wings and confessed he had forgotten to get the stuff for the bubbles. Mike leapt up with a roar and ordered him to go to all the delicatessen shops open all night around Broadway and buy every box of detergent available. When the prop man eventually returned, he emptied the boxes into the tank. As the cold water rushed in, the girls squealed in shock, and the bubbles slowly started to rise. They grew like cloud banks, submerging the shrieking girls who thought they were going to drown. We watched, mesmerized, as the billows of bubbles overflowed the tank, crept over the stage and heaved over into the orchestra pit. The musicians fled gripping their instruments, some drenched by the descending blanket of evaporating bubbles. Although the stagehands had turned off the water, the bubbles continued to multiply. When the girls

Gypsy Rose Lee, Karinska, Sharaff. *Harper's Bazaar*, July, 1942. Photograph by Louise Dahl-Wolfe. Courtesy *Harper's Bazaar*.

THE NEW YORK TIMES, MONDAY, MAY 1, 1950.

Thailand's Orchestra-Leading King Writes Songs for Broadway Show

Phumiphon Aduldet, 22-year-old King of Thailand, who is American-born and interested in musical composition, will be represented on Broadway in a forthcoming revue, it was learned yesterday.

"Blue Night," a song by the youthful monarch, will be featured in a production number in "Michael Todd's Peep Show," along with a medley of five other songs written by the King. Going into rehearsal tomorrow, the show is due to open here on June 21 after a three-week tryout in Philadelphia. The King has expressly stipulated that all royalties from his songs shall go to the Royal Thailand Charities.

Just how Mr. Todd, the perennial boy wonder of show business, managed to bridge the gap between Thailand and Broadway was not fully disclosed. Enough details were learned, however, to indicate that the producer had had to bring all his powers of persuasion and showmanship to bear in obtaining the King's consent to have his songs go into the show.

Negotiations were carried on by cable between Mr. Todd and Prince Chakraband, the King's Chamberlain, who apparently is also his business manager.

Mr. Todd, when in Europe last February, heard that the Thailand monarch wrote popular songs. But he soon found out that getting the King to agree to have his songs in a Broadway show was a different matter.

There Mr. Todd's early training as a salesman stood him in good stead. He called the King's attention to the fact that President Truman played the piano and that his daughter Margaret appeared on the concert platform. The clincher came, it was learned, when Mr. Todd used Andrew Fletcher's seventeenth-century observation about the making of a nation's laws being somewhat subordinate to the making of a nation's songs.

(Bartlett's "Familiar Quotations" gives it as: "Give me the making of the songs of a nation, and I

Continued on Page 12, Column 4

Continued From Page 1

care not who makes its laws." Stevenson's "Home Book of Quotations" has the phrasing, taken from a letter written by Fletcher to the Marquis of Montrose, as "If a man were permitted to make all the ballads, he need not fear who should make the laws of a nation.")

Mr. Todd's resourcefulness brought final fruit when on April 10 he received a cable at his Broadway Theatre offices from Prince Chakraband advising him that his terms were acceptable. The songs, sent by air mail, were written in both English and Siamese. The music was by the King and he was assisted in writing the lyrics by Prince Chakraband. "Blue Night" was described by a songwriting expert as a "sensuous beguine" and the other songs were said to be character pieces or ballads.

Mr. Todd's office said that the producer had obtained the English publication and production rights to all the King's songs. The producer declined to comment on any aspect of the King's song writing. "I defer to His Majesty," he said.

King Phumiphon was reported yesterday to be honeymooning at a seaside resort in Thailand with his bride, the 17-year-old Princess Sirikit Kitiyakara. They were married in Bangkok last Friday.

The young King was born in 1927 in a Cambridge, Mass., hospital when his father, Prince Mahidol, was studying medicine at Harvard. He spent his early years at Brookline, Mass.

King Phumiphon plays the piano, drums and the horn and likes to lead orchestras. His bride also plays the piano. Among their wedding gifts were a console radio-phonograph from President and Mrs. Truman.

King Phumiphon
Associated Press

Article in *The New York Times*, May 1, 1950. © 1950 The New York Times Co. Reprinted by permission. Photograph: Wide World Photos.

Show girl. *Peepshow*.

were finally rescued from the tank, they emerged bright green, for the painters had failed to use waterproof paint on the tank.

Long before rehearsals, however, and at the end of a production meeting at Mike's office with Hassard Short, the director, and Howard Bay, the scenic designer, I showed Mike a copy of *Time* magazine in which the cover story was about the King of Siam, who was a jazz buff. He played the clarinet, had a private orchestra, and had composed many pop songs. Mike glanced through the article and yelled for his secretary. He immediately dictated a cable to the King of Siam — the nerviest and funniest cable I have ever heard — asking His Majesty to write a song specially for *Peepshow*. Hassard, Howard, and I never expected anything to happen, but in three days a cable came announcing that the new musical composition was en route. Mike was of course jubilant. The story made the front page of *The New York Times*, and the subsequent publicity enabled him to raise the rest of the backing and put the show into rehearsal.

The title of the King's song was "Blue Night." In substance it had much in common with the typical Tin Pan Alley product. Mike, however, on the scent of continuing publicity and eager to give full scope to the composition, had the music orchestrated till it sounded like a tone poem. The results proved painful all around. On opening night the Siamese ambassador, in a box draped with Siamese and American flags, sat deadpan through the whole show and wholly impassive throughout the King's composition.

As for the costumes for the "Blue Night" number, months before I knew I would work on *Peepshow* or that there would be a Siamese number, I had seen in *Art News* magazine a photograph of a Siamese weaver displaying some materials he had woven. I cut out the picture in case by some lucky chance I would be able to use them. When "Blue Night" offered this opportunity I tracked down Thaibok, a small shop in the basement of a brownstone on Sixty-first Street, and found there some of the loveliest swatches of colors I had ever seen.

Thaibok was much more than a shop. It was the outlet in New York for a concern in Bangkok set up by Jim Thompson. In Thailand during the Second World War Jim had met a Laotian refugee who, with a group of weavers, was producing a small amount of materials of both Laotian and Thai designs. He became associated with this project. Under his guidance dyes were made sunfast, the material woven in marketable widths, some of the designs modified, and new ones introduced based on old patterns.

When I met Jim about a week after my first visit to the shop, he suggested flying back to Bangkok to have some materials woven for the number. Unfortunately this was not possible in time for the costumes to be made. Unfortunately, too, the stock in the shop was low and very few pieces of what I wanted available in enough yardage. I did use a few pieces of Thaibok material for the first time, choosing silks of gold and bronze tones, deep purple and acid greens and pinks. Later on, while I was designing *The King and I*, Jim and I worked closely together on colors and patterns for the silks which were woven in Bangkok and brought to New York.

In the four different productions of *The King and I* — the original Rodgers and Hammerstein production on Broadway in 1951, the London edition at the

Drury Lane Theatre in 1953, the 20th Century-Fox film of 1956, and the Lincoln Center revival in 1964 — a great deal of Thai silk was used, as well as Chinese damasks and brocades, cloth woven in India, Japan, and Hong Kong, and some thin cottons printed by silk-screening in New York. While these materials sound sumptuous and a great deal of yardage was used, I was able to bring the costumes of the original production in well under the budget.

A Broadway production was a fine showcase for the work of the Thai weavers, and after *Peepshow* and particularly after *The King and I* opened on Broadway, decorators and designers began to use the silks in increasing volume. At first, Thaibok could not keep up with the demand. However, soon it moved to larger quarters in New York and was able also to supply firms in London and Paris.

6. Placing costumes in period, place, character/Handling colors for stage and screen

Before becoming involved in Siamese clothes of the 1860s, I had been learning as much as possible about costumes of various periods and countries: the different silhouettes, the cut and fit, the lines and proportions, the range and combinations of colors. One had to know as much as possible about the characteristics of clothes before translating them into whatever might be required on stage. In some plays a literalness is suitable and it is a matter of adaptation, though color and detail should contribute to characterization and to the moods of the play. In others, and particularly musicals, a freer interpretation — including one's own comment — is possible and in fact works best.

The "Easter Parade" number followed fairly faithfully the fashions of 1885, though the palette of browns had to be worked out carefully. In that other newspaper number, "The Girl on *The Police Gazette*," there was complete freedom to design costumes for Gypsy and the show girls to make them pretty and provocative, and the entire number in variations on the pink and black turned out feminine, charming, and with a certain elegance. Another opportunity to key a number in one basic color was in *Magdalena*, an operetta with a score by the Brazilian composer Villa-Lobos. Set in Latin America and with some scenes in Paris, the time about 1911, there were certain requirements in the Paris and period costumes, and the clothes of the tribe living along the Magdalena River had a uniformity in silhouette and proportions — including derby hats worn by the women — that had to be followed fairly closely. The freedom in designing the costumes was in the colors and there was opportunity for gaiety and drama. In the production number at the edge of the jungle, the singers and dancers, the entire ensemble of the large company, poured slowly on stage in every hue and tone conceivable of red. Underlying the music of the orchestra and the voices, the reds sang out in unison. This saturation of reds and the power in color were never more vividly illustrated for me than in that number.

George Kaufman and Edna Ferber's *The Land is Bright* was a rather ambitious chronicle of a family from about 1900 to the mid-thirties. The costumes had to indicate the passage of time and changes of fortune. Lighthearted musicals such as Ed Wynn's *Boys and Girls Together* and Eddie Cantor's *Banjo Eyes* called for contemporary clothes and costumes. *Lady in the Dark* in 1941 was also contemporary. With the book by Moss Hart, music by Kurt Weill, and lyrics by Ira Gershwin, Gertrude Lawrence scintillated. In the circus number in this show Danny Kaye as the ringmaster recited his famous patter song of composers' names, and Victor Mature as a lion tamer in full-length tights dyed shocking pink and short trunks of tiger skin also sang and was sensational.

The Great Waltz, set in Vienna in the 1860s, about Johann Strauss and his music was naturally a lovely romantic show to design. Oscar Hammerstein and Sigmund Romberg's *Sunny River* was romance in New Orleans during the Empire period. *White Horse Inn* was Tyrolean and set in idyllic times. Moss Hart and Cole Porter's *Jubilee*, focusing on England and King George V and Queen Mary, included a production number, a fete which required ancient Cretan and Greek costumes. Apparently, at the time, this did not surprise me, though now that I think of it, I can not imagine why and conclude that the number was arrived at through the odd reasoning that sometimes occurs in the world of theater.

Costumes based on ancient Greek clothes took over the stage in two musicals I designed at this time: in 1938, *The Boys from Syracuse*, the Rodgers and Hart musical based on *A Comedy of Errors*, in which Eddie Albert and Jimmy Savo starred; and in 1942, *By Jupiter*, with Ray Bolger, Constance Moore, and Benay Venuta. While the settings of both shows were supposed to be ancient Greece, the light mood of the plays required not authentic costumes but ones which made use of certain elements of classical Greek dress: the pleated chiton, the characteristic draping or folding of material over a shoulder or around the body, the ribboned sandals the thongs of which were crisscrossed on some legs from ankle to just below the knee. The Phrygian cap (not a Greek style, though depicted in ancient Greek art), used pervasively in *By Jupiter*, and the fillet around heads used in both these shows, were originally good basic design, so that from time to time one sees them adapted in contemporary fashion.

One tends to associate the colors of Greek clothes in ancient times with the statues we have seen and think of them as white and remarkably unsoiled; the terracotta red and black of the urns might also come to mind. But the colors were as bright and various as anywhere else at any time. They probably soon lost intensity since mineral and vegetable dyes were used, which fade quickly. For one group of costumes in *By Jupiter* I used a rich crimson, rose carthame, and a deep forest green, delighted for a moment in what seemed to be a new combination but realizing almost immediately that this was a team of colors used in the Renaissance. Most people who work with forms and colors automatically note variations and tones, and find that what they have observed, particularly forms and colors that have given them pleasure, get imprinted at some level of memory and have a way of surfacing unpredictably from "the storehouse mind."

A clansman in the film *Brigadoon*.

Turban of a dancer in *Scheherazade* ballet, *On Your Toes*.

An Incroyable wig, basis of wigs in *Scheherazade* take-off.

Mata Hari's costume in the Java sequence. *Mata Hari*. Photograph by Alfredo de Molli.

The emotional impact of color in costumes designed for stage or screen is direct and immediate. It can help or detract from a scene, can set the tone of an entire production number, can add to a characterization by actor or actress, and give that extra zip to a dancer. In the days of the Civic and with each show on Broadway I learned a bit more about how colors behave, the somber and the bright, those that blend in contrast to the clashing, and the infinite range of tones that can appear on a palette.

Color has always been important to me. I dream in color more often than in black and white; people and situations are symbolized for me by colors; numerals and words have color. I remember my surprise in childhood — like "the shock of recognition" — on reading a poem that began "Goodbye is a yellow ribboned word," for that was how I had imagined it. The names themselves of colors have poetry, the reds perhaps the loveliest: scarlet, vermilion, rose carthame, garance, incarnadine, and so on, playing on eye and ear.

There is an aspect of color which might be classed as national. In Europe, for instance, certain colors seem to represent French taste; the Italian sense of color is characteristically richer and more daring; the clear light blue of the sky over Athens may have suggested the basic color of one of the two Greek flags, and though we associate it with Eton blue, it is definitely a Greek hue. The English, until recently, were extremely restrained in the use of color, excepting — characteristically — the dress uniforms of famous regiments before khaki took over. After the Second World War, however, they began to play with color as though they had just discovered it. In Asia, color like everything else is rooted in beliefs and ritual. Even with the rapid changes affecting traditional practices, white is still the color of mourning, red naturally associated with joy and happiness, blue the color for scholars and students, and yellow worn by priests and monks.

There is considerable difference between choosing and handling colors in designing costumes for the movies and for the theater. Colors behave differently on film than they do under stage lighting.

In the theater one has to take into account how colors are affected by lighting from footlights, overhead and side lights. Projected through various colored gelatines (red, blue, amber, white or clear, and "surprise pink"), lighting can enhance or kill the visual effects on a stage, depending on the lighting specialist's skill in balancing the lights through the colored gelatines. Too much amber can turn red into brown and blue and green into muddy colors; amber, of course, intensifies warm yellows, but can cancel the effect of cool yellows. "Surprise pink" perks up the whole color scale and is the light actors and actresses after a certain age love for its flattering aura. The use of blue gelatines with the others helps to "normalize" the whole range of colors. Red, alone, is used only for occasional special effects.

Leslie Uggams' rubies and pheasant feathers in nightclub number, *Hallelujah, Baby!*

In handling colors in films, one has to consider the high intensity of lights on a set, sometimes heightened by reflectors, which are capable of washing out colors; or, as is becoming more frequent, natural light outdoors with or without the aid of reflectors. Then, assuming that the colors planned for the costumes are appropriate to the character, scene, and period, one has to keep in mind how colors behave on film. This involves first the cameraman's eye and taste, and what can happen to color in a long shot, medium shot, or close-up — to name the minimum basic shots, and the kind of lighting of the various shots. Next, the technical steps of processing the footage of film to the final print. Of course, by then a designer has no control over the colors, and certainly there is no possibility to make changes.

Even at the last step, when the film is being run for an audience, colors can vary a great deal depending on the print. For each print is processed separately in the laboratory, the timing and exposure of each print determined largely according to skin tones and aiming for the most natural facial tones. An audience may see what is called a "red print," in which that color will dominate and faces sometimes have the appearance of a severe sunburn. Or it may be a "green print" in which case faces often look ashen or slightly sick in the general pervading greenish bluish tint. I have seen a glorious spectrum of pinks to reds of billowing satin skirts on a line of show girls, which I designed for a number in *Guys and Dolls*, come out in one print looking liverish, quite repulsive, and nowhere near the colors used. Another print, seen at another time, approximated the colors fairly closely.

Boy dancer in the ballet *PAMTGG* ("Pan-Am makes the going great").

Girl dancer in the ballet *PAMTGG*.

Potentate. Ballet in the film *An American in Paris*.

Three women. "Big Spender" number in Broadway musical *Sweet Charity*.

Four dancers. "Integration" number in Broadway musical *Hallelujah, Baby*.

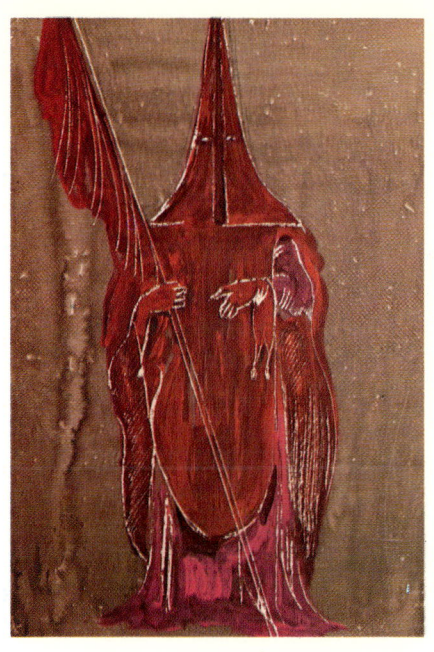

Executioner. "Inquisition" sequence in Broadway musical *Candide*.

Tuptim (headdress). Film, *The King and I*.

Group of dancers. Ballet, *Age of Anxiety*.

Three officers. South American sequence in Broadway musical *Candide*.

Two women. *I Picked a Daisy,* a musical projected for Broadway in 1962.

Justine. Burnoose worn in riding scene in the film *Justine*.

Kate. Wedding banquet scene in the film *The Taming of the Shrew*.

Lady Thiang. Film, *The King and I*.

Kate. Wedding night scene in the film *The Taming of the Shrew*.

Two costers. London street number celebrating the Coronation, in Broadway musical *The Girl Who Came to Supper*.

Two women. Film, *Porgy and Bess*.

Ellie. Café-opening scene in the film *The Great White Hope*.

Leopard and lion. "Adam and Eve" ballet in the film *Can-Can*.

Three dancers. Ballet in the Broadway musical *Flower Drum Song*.

Two dancers. "Slaughter on Tenth Avenue" ballet in the Broadway musical *On Your Toes*.

Dancers. South American sequence in the Broadway musical *Candide*.

Show girl. "Traviata" number in the film *Ziegfeld Follies*.

Films shot in color have long passed the experimental stage and are now so completely taken for granted that a black-and-white or a sepia-toned movie appears unusual and even innovative. When the process was still being perfected, the medium was used for every film possible and of course for musicals. The studios were at first rather awed by the medium. Soon, however, they began to regard not only the new process but also the natural phenomenon of color as Hollywood inventions.

I learned by trial and error what colors to avoid. Some of them which photographed badly were in the family of the blue greens, for even a pale turquoise can appear so bright that it shrieks on film. The three-color process is made up of the primary colors, in strips of red, yellow, and blue; but the cyan dye used for the blue is so strong that it bleeds through the other two and intensifies any tone related to it. If the bright blue sky in a movie sometimes seems overpowering for no obvious purpose, it could be due to the cyan blue, and there is nothing that can be done to control it. For the same reason a clear green is very difficult to achieve in costumes, for it comes out either too blue or too yellow. As for red, unless the shades of red are used alone or next to a green they will generally appear murky.

A controlled and fairly muted palette seems the most successful, for in the processing of film the colors are automatically intensified. After experimenting with various shades and tones, I learned to gauge the degree of color to use so that the final results on film appeared the way I wanted them to. Moreover, cameramen prefer muted colors because they are easier to light; and when the film is being processed, low-keyed colors are more easily regulated in the general balancing of the colors.

Pure white always invites protest from cameramen and is a problem to the technicians who process the film. For when it is photographed, light tends to bounce off it, causing a disturbing iridescence which cannot be eliminated in the processing. When color processing was being developed, technicians experimented with various whites to determine how to control this phenomenon. Some soft hues of pale gray or beige can be made to look white, the degree of whiteness depending on where and how the white is used, under what lighting, and in relation to which other colors.

In the oral shorthand used among those working with color in films, sometimes before a shot, white is requires to be "teched" or lowered according to a number. This refers to a white numbered on a chart covering the whole scale of whites. After a shot, technicians on a set will say, "Take a lily." This calls for the shot of a board on which there are innumerable squares of grays ranging from white to black used to gauge the relative tones of colors, so that this gauge for the technicians is put on the film immediately following the scene which has been shot.

7. MGM in the forties/Adrian/ *Meet Me in St. Louis*/ Designing and shooting schedules/ Changing role of designers

For many years Metro-Goldwyn-Mayer made most of the musicals in Hollywood. In 1942 Arthur Freed asked me to work in his unit there. I was one among several whom he brought to Hollywood from Broadway.

As it happened, however, the first movie at MGM for which I designed costumes was not a musical but *Madame Curie*, in black and white. Greer Garson and Walter Pidgeon starred, in a sincere Hollywood attempt to tell the heroic story of the two Curies. It was a welcome change from Broadway musicals. It also gave me a chance to learn about the medium of film, and to get acquainted with Adrian, who for over twenty-five years had been the chief costume designer at MGM and had left to open his fashion salon in Beverly Hills.

More than any other designer in show business at the time Adrian had influenced fashion. We had a strong bond in common in that both of us had been given our first chance to design on Broadway by Hassard Short, and under similar circumstances. For Hassard had seen Adrian's sketches just after he had finished art school and had asked him to do the costumes for a number in Hassard's *Music Box Revue*.

The first evening I spent with Adrian and his wife Janet Gaynor, on entering the room I felt that I had stepped on to a MGM set. Like an underwater grotto, everything seemed to be pale blue and green. Above the fireplace, however, was a lovely seventeenth-century overmantel carved in fruitwood. It was a work of Grinling Gibbons, and one of the few major pieces by the master carver in a private collection in this country.

Adrian told me a great deal about what it had been like when he started at MGM. He spoke of being summoned to Louis B. Mayer's office whenever a costume or even a detail did not completely meet his approval. Louis B. Mayer, as he seems usually to have been called, or with that finer shade of familiarity so important in Hollywood simply "L. B.", was one of the legendary moguls in the movie industry. I did not see Mr. Mayer often. In fact, I was in his office only once: when Lem Ayers and I showed him the scenery and costume designs for *Meet Me in St. Louis*. The few times I met him on the midway — the Main Street of MGM along which were offices, some of the departments, dressing rooms, and sound-stages — he stopped to greet me, patted my shoulder, and invariably announced, "I've just made the greatest picture, Miss Sharaff, and the next will be even greater!"

Adrian also told me how he had arrived at using shoulder pads, a feature that became like his signature on clothes he designed. It seems that Joan Crawford insisted on feeling absolutely free in her dresses and suits. At fittings she would rotate her shoulders vigorously, with arms outstretched, to test the stretch of the garment across her shoulder blades. As this feeling of unhampered freedom in clothes is possible only in loose jersey or a sweater, all other fabrics Adrian used for her clothes had to be let out across the back to such an extent that padding was necessary on the shoulders to take up the slack. The result accentuated her own broad and angular shoulders. With each outfit Adrian designed for her, the shoulders became increasingly exaggerated. As Crawford was one of the leading stars and of glamourous repute, her silhouette became a pattern, soon copied, and for ten years shoulder pads were the outstanding item manufactured in the fashion industry.

The Crawford silhouette exaggerating the shoulders was a step that was perhaps sooner or later inevitable in women's fashions. For the fluctuations of fashion tend to emphasize one or another part of the body and to alter its proportions. Adrian's focusing on the shoulders was gradually replaced by a new concentration on the bosom. When I started to work in Hollywood, there was no star or starlet who did not know the exact size of the padding she thought she needed in her bra to be sexy. The word "sexy" was synonymous with the size of the bosom. One result was that most of the young actresses clamored for more and more padding and ended up looking as though they were supporting the Himalayas across the chest.

About five thousand people worked at MGM in the forties and the various departments were scattered all over the studio. The prop department was a fabulous area filled over the years in the past by buyers sent to Europe to pick up period pieces of all sorts. There were huge Spanish armoires, eighteenth-century grillwork, suits and pieces of armor and weapons, furniture and objects of various periods, chandeliers, candlelabras, sets of china, Georgian silver tea sets — all now dispersed. There were, of course, also many things less splendid and less valuable, stored in case they might be needed. Tucked in a corner was a dining room set Louis B. Mayer had ordered specially from China: a table with several leaves and about two dozen chairs elaborately carved with dragons rampant and tinted with color and gold leaf.

Attached to the prop department was the plaster shop, where practically anything could be made, including such things as suckling pigs and poultry sprayed to the perfect mouthwatering shade. Served on platters and accompanied by numerous other dishes, they were courses in gargantuan feasts staged in some movies in the past. Some extraordinarily talented sculptors and craftsmen worked in this department.

Another group of various talents at the studio at that time gathered at lunch at the writers' table in the commissary. I trespassed almost daily on this writers' island because the talk was generally entertaining, ranging from the sort of morose gloom in which writers in that kind of captivity seem to indulge to occasionally sharp exchanges, ribaldry, wisecracks, and fleeting wit. Among the writers there were James Cain, Robert Nathan, Sonya Levien, Mary McCall, Isobel Lennart, and briefly Tennessee Williams, Bella Spewack, and the loquacious Katherine Anne Porter with her special talent and star sapphire eyes. Jules Dassin, who was then a director at MGM, also chose to sit at the writers' table, eschewing the table reserved for the upper echelon of the producers and directors.

For the actresses, the three most important departments were hairdressing, make-up, and costume — in that order. In the first two, face and hair were studied and analyzed. Compared to make-up in the theater, these men in the studio's make-up department worked like skillful miniaturists. They were, however, usually so intent on ironing out deficiencies, even the natural asymmetry of a face, that in most instances final results presented an unreal image, either too good to be genuine or emptied of individuality. The hairdresser reigned supreme. Disregarding whether a hairdo was appropriate or whether it went with the face, his main concern was to invent a hairstyle that would attract attention, lend glamour to his name, keep him in constant demand, and, he hoped, initiate a new fashion.

One section of the make-up department dealt with character actors and had developed the art of make-up to an extraordinary degree. It was organized with such efficiency that, for instance, drawer upon drawer containing rows of differently shaped ears filled cabinets along one wall of a room; the exact cauliflower ear for an actor could be fished out pronto.

The attitude which made actresses depend to such an extreme on make-up men and hairdressers, and which put such great value on youth, sometimes was exaggerated ridiculously. At one time children of stars were not mentioned or allowed to appear with their star parents in person or in photographs. Until Dietrich broke the taboo, no star would admit to being a grandparent. Motherhood, to say nothing of grandmotherhood, was associated with gray hair. In one of the first movies I watched being filmed, the star was dismayed over having an eight-year-old son in the picture. The hairdresser, leaving her face untouched by the years, sprayed her hair a silver gray so the audience would accept her as a mother.

The hurdles set up by censorship then seem incredible today. There were strict rules decreeing exactly how much of the body could be exposed. Nudity in films being accepted now without a second thought, it seems unbelievable that even in the 1940s women's bathing suits could not be made without a skirt attached. With the emphasis on bosoms at the time, the amount of cleavage permitted was left to the discretion of a man from the censorship office, whose OK was necessary for every dress and costume before it could be shot. I was visiting on a set when a censor was on the job: a small gray man, serious and stern at his task, he stood in front of Lana Turner's well-padded bosom peering down her low-cut dress. Shaking his head, he turned to the designer standing anxiously beside him and said, "You'd better cover the cleavage with net or tulle. It'll never pass the office." This taboo on crannies and expanses of flesh started a prodigious use in Hollywood of nude-colored souffle under transparent materials, for so long as there was a covering, however thin, the studio could claim that the actress was fully clothed.

In 1943 when I worked on my first musical production at MGM, Arthur Freed's *Meet Me in St. Louis,* technicolor was established but the large screen was not yet in use. The movie may now seem an old-fashioned musical, but when it was made it was hailed as a breakthrough. Music and songs were closely integrated with the story, which was mainly about a family in St. Louis in 1905. Reversing the usual, the heroine sang about the boy next door. And no one up till then had thought to write a song about a trolley car. It was an attempt not only to have the music and songs help tell the story but also to get nearer to ordinary life.

Realism in movies at that time was still largely of the brand popularly associated with Hollywood, with its peculiar air of the unreal. Audiences enjoyed and apparently wanted this kind of exaggeration, slickness, superficiality, and the heavy dose of saccharine. Who had seen a king-size bed before it appeared in a movie? Or satin sheets? A star playing the role of a secretary of modest means changed her dress and matching accessories for every scene. Audiences were conditioned to expect an ingenue to be the Hollywood prototype. All leading ladies, however ordinary or drab or impoverished the character in the story, were coiffed and clothed immaculately, made up to the nines, and had perfect teeth. The hero was of course just as gorgeous. The regular, gleaming white teeth of movie stars undoubtedly gave a big boost to dentistry.

The edging towards realism in movies was slow but continuous. I recall a remark made by Doc Merman of 20th Century-Fox during *Cleopatra* in 1961. In his characteristically gravelled voice he said, "Nowadays everything in movies has to be for real. People want to see real houses, real streets, even real blood when somebody's killed. That wasn't the way we used to make movies!" Since then, we have moved to a curious contradiction between the means and the material — to an expert documentary style that is used increasingly for the extremes and distortions of sensationalism, which in turn raises questions about what is entertaining and what is real in entertainment. Watching some of "the way we used to make movies" while functioning as a designer, such questions were being formed for me in those years at MGM when one balked at many aspects of what is ambiguously lumped together under the name "Hollywood."

Returning to the attempt at period realism in *Meet Me in St. Louis*, the costumes of 1905 at first dismayed the producer. When he saw the sketches, even though the style had been modified, Freed's pained remark was, "How can you have a star with no cleavage?" When I explained the mono-bosom look of the period, he replied that it would be fine for the mother, but Judy Garland could not possibly wear it. Judy's costumes in the movie had tightly fitted bodices. Mary Astor, who played her mother, was pleased from the start with her costumes, accepted the silhouette, wore her costumes with style, and looked extremely well in them, particularly in the last scene. In it, she was in a white dress and hat and carried a parasol, and was surrounded by four daughters, also in white, as the family set out for the Fair.

Judy Garland in the Fair scene. From the MGM release *Meet Me in St. Louis* © 1944. Copyright renewed 1971 Metro-Goldwyn-Mayer.

Mary Astor in the Fair scene. From the MGM release *Meet Me in St. Louis* © 1944. Copyright renewed 1971 Metro-Goldwyn-Mayer.

Costume sketch of Mary Astor's dress in the Fair scene.

The four daughters off to the Fair. From the MGM release *Meet Me in St. Louis* © 1944. Copyright renewed 1971 Metro-Goldwyn-Mayer.

Because of the war, materials were very scarce, and since period clothes depend a great deal on the kind of fabric, I had to invent substitutes for some outfits. For Mary Astor's white dress in the finale I got a strong net in fairly large mesh and had small silk leaves sewn over it, which were then appliquéd with tiny satin buttons and thin silk tendrils. Watching the step by step execution of this costume, I was impressed by the expertise of the seamstresses; when the dress was finished, it looked as though it had been made of handmade Venetian lace. Since Mary's husband in the story was presumably a solid and successful citizen, and the Fair was a once-in-a-lifetime festive occasion, the dress was appropriate, with the necessary degree of theatricality for a musical. What is more, it gave Mary a happy feeling which showed in the radiance she gave that scene.

In working on *Meet Me in St. Louis* I experienced for the first time some of the extreme contrasts between preparing for a production in films and one in the theater, particularly in the time element and the scheduling.

The time that a costume designer has to prepare for a musical in the theater usually averages two to three weeks on the sketches for about two-thirds of the show, plus about three weeks of fittings during which the rest of the sketches are made. The economics of theater production put tremendous pressure on every department. For the costumes the three fittings allowed by union rules and the production office have to be squeezed into the rehearsal schedule. Dancers and singers are usually hired right up to and often during rehearsals and cannot be fitted for costumes until they get the jobs. Changes in the script and sometimes of the cast, additional songs or numbers, and occasionally drastic changes of story and characters made during the out-of-town runs, all affect the designing and the making of the costumes. Changes may be cuts in the script or of songs or numbers, which can mean a waste of time, production dollars, designs, materials, and the energies of the people in the workrooms.

There is more time in getting the costumes ready for a movie. The pace, though at times frenetic, never gets as frenzied as in the theater. This is fortunate, particularly because costumes open to scrutiny in close-ups, medium shots (from waist up), and the "two-shot" (between a close-up and a medium shot) have to be made more carefully, with greater attention to fit, detail, and finish. In the perspective of the theater auditorium, figures on the stage are always seen full length and as a whole, thus broader effects are more suitable. In movies, with the various camera shots and because colors of costumes come out better on film when they are lowered in tone, a costume generally needs less exaggeration and theatricality.

The amount of work that sometimes goes into making a costume for a movie may seem disparate to its relatively brief appearance on film, but it is a fact that just as the technical means of making movies have been perfected, so too audiences' eyes have become keener and more demanding. Film makers accordingly have to be reasonably sure that anything slipshod is avoided. A theater audience is generally more lenient about costume details; but almost everyone in a movie audience considers himself a critic. As mail to the studios used to show, and as even casual conversations still show, people have opinions about every aspect of a movie.

One obvious advantage in movies is that, once on film, costumes remain unchanged. If a costume is meant to look fresh, it retains that freshness. In the theater, costumes, particularly in musicals, worn six evenings and two matinees week in and week out, take a terrific beating. Many have to stand up to quick changes. They must be made durable and cannot escape being sewn rather heavy-handedly. Less durable than scenery, costumes in the theater are among the first parts of a production to begin to show wear and tear.

Most of the costume sketches for a large-scale musical do not have to be done before the shooting starts. They are usually made in the period before and during the first part of the shooting. When tests are called for, specific costumes for stars and leading players are prepared in time for the brief shots of walking back and forth, turning, and sitting before the camera.

The shooting schedule holds a company together and guides the making of the film from day to day. Worked out by the production staff, it is flexible to allow for contingencies but holds the production in line and keeps it moving steadily on its course. A sheet of a day's shooting is generally issued the day before. The schedule is not made according to the sequence of scenes in the script or in chronological order. Many factors determine its planning — too numerous and in some cases too technical to go into here — but the building of sets and availability of actors are two basic considerations. For instance, a set that is ready at a certain date might call for shooting on it of a sequence of scenes and also other, separate scenes in the script that take place in the same setting. There may be occasion to shoot all the scenes in which a particular actor appears, or conversely, to shoot around a star — that is, scenes in which he or she does not appear. Weather is another factor which has to be taken into account for outdoor scenes, although weather is less disrupting in California than on location abroad, where it can be unpredictable. Certain indoor scenes are kept in readiness to substitute for outdoor shooting in case of sudden weather changes.

As to how the shooting schedule applies to costumes, the first step in making a breakdown or list of costumes required in a film is usually made by the business office of the wardrobe department. The designer then breaks this down according to the shooting schedule so as to know what is to be designed and when it will be needed. While the shooting schedule does not follow the sequence of scenes as they are in the script, the designer must keep both time and scene sequence clearly in mind. An actor cannot appear in an outfit in one scene on a set and walk through a door on to another set for a sequence to the scene (which may be shot before or long after the first) dressed in a different outfit. Although the wardrobe people check before each scene and the script girl on the set notes every detail in the shooting script scene by scene as it is shot, the designer is responsible for providing the complete costumes when they are scheduled. For *Cleopatra*, in which I designed sixty costumes for Elizabeth Taylor, I started using a chart to help keep things clear. It covered one wall of the small office, was useful for the color plan, and served also to tell at a glance which costumes and accessories had been shot, which were needed next, and which would be called for later. From then on I used charts for all large productions.

One fundamental difference which I found at MGM in 1942 between designing costumes for the screen and for the stage illustrates a step in the changing role of designers. At that time there was an almost Victorian attitude in the separation of designing of men's costumes from those of the women. There was also a division of labor between designing for the stars — mainly the female stars — and for the supporting players, and further, between their costumes and those for the extras. Designers like Adrian, who started in the era of silent pictures, Travis Banton, and Orry Kelly were renowned for their costumes for leading ladies. They designed almost exclusively for women stars. Other designers worked on the costumes for the men and for the supporting players. The extras were clothed by the wardrobe department. Apart from lists, hardly any attention was given to integrating the costumes of stars with the others, and little thought was given to a degree of coherence in the look of a scene and of the production as a whole. No one designer was assigned to do an entire movie and made responsible for the final results.

Accustomed to the Broadway pattern, I took for granted that designing the costumes for a production meant all of the clothes in it. When Arthur Freed brought me to Hollywood, I believe he had some idea of applying the Broadway pattern and trying for a unified approach in the costumes through the whole picture. Our discussions over my sketches, which covered all of the actors and actresses in the movie, always took in the scene or number as a whole in the context of the entire film. It was the business manager of the wardrobe department who was taken aback by my designing the men's as well as the women's clothes. When he handed me the breakdowns, first for *Madame Curie* and then for *Meet Me in St. Louis*, and I asked where the lists of men's clothes were, we were both astonished — in different ways — when he explained the usual procedure. Then and thereafter, except in the few instances when I have been assigned specifically to design a star's costumes or one or two numbers in a musical which were equivalent to a whole production, I have always done all of the costumes in a production. The situation began to change in Hollywood, and I believe it soon became generally accepted that one designer was put on a picture and worked on all of the costumes in it.

8. Back and forth between Broadway and Hollywood

In the background of stage and screen productions there are the unions. The size of the membership among the numerous unions, their regulations, and their actions vary greatly. In general, however, no one can function in show business unless he or she is a paying member of a union. Scenic and costume designers in New York are a relatively small group in a union whose unwieldy name, like a huge umbrella, covers a multitude of crafts: the United Scenic Artists Local Union 829 of the Brotherhood of Painters, Decorators, and Paperhangers of America. When I started in the theater, there were three women in our union — Gladys Calthrop, Aline Bernstein, and myself. As a very young and green member, I spoke up at one meeting and was promptly squelched by a burly fellow member shouting across the room "Shut up, Brother Sharaff!" Since then, the number of designers and women designers in the membership has of course greatly increased, and euphemistically speaking, "all men are brothers."

In Hollywood, until the Costume Designers' Guild was formed in 1953, there was no union of this branch of movie production. In the mid-forties, five scenic and costume designers from Broadway working at various studios were caught in a strike. The strike had nothing to do with designers, but was essentially a test of power by a Hollywood union: in one of its periodic muscle-flexing it was attempting to organize the office personnel in the movie studios. The union in New York decided to make a grand gesture across the three thousand miles of America by pulling the five of us out on a "sympathy" strike — and incidentally out of our jobs. We were ordered to appear before a panel of the Hollywood union, which behaved with no signs of fraternity but like a judge and jury dealing with criminals. As things happened, and in a few weeks, the secretaries, and others in the offices who had not wanted to belong to the union remained as they were, and the five designers were left suspended half in and half out of jobs. At MGM I had worked for Arthur Freed on *Yolanda and the Thief*, a musical based on a story by Ludwig Bemelmans, and on the "Traviata" and "Limehouse" numbers in

Ziegfeld Follies. Officially, if one went on strike while under contract to a studio, even the short sympathy strike for which we had been the puny token, the contract automatically ended. As it turned out, I went to work on three Broadway shows in succession before coming back to Hollywood the next year.

Billion Dollar Baby, a musical set in the twenties, written by Betty Comden and Adolph Green, with a memorable score by Morton Gould and choreography by Jerome Robbins, was perhaps ahead of its time, for audiences after the war were in no mood to enjoy a story about the crash, bootleggers, and gangsters. The costumes were, however, fun to design. I had raccoon coats made with loops of wool sprayed to look like the fur; to my eyes, bell-bottom trousers and short straight dresses seemed surprisingly modern; I invented evening dresses that resembled Japanese paper bells, and transparent cloche hats through which could be seen the short haircuts with bangs of the chorus girls.

The other two shows were straight plays produced by the versatile Mike Todd: the *G. I. Hamlet* in modern clothes starring Maurice Evans, and *The Would-Be Gentleman*, Mike's other reach among the classics to do a period camp of *Le Bourgeois Gentilhomme* with Bobby Clark in the leading role, unforgettable as his eyes ringed by painted-on goggles popped in surprise at speaking prose. Returning to Hollywood, I went to work for Sam Goldwyn.

In the small independent studio, where one picture at a time was made, the atmosphere was almost cosy. Sam, as the producer, had direct and daily contact with the people working at his studio. Among the four pictures I worked on there, which were all contemporary stories, two were reunions with Danny Kaye: James Thurber's *The Secret Life of Walter Mitty* and a musical, *A Song is Born*. Like a Goldwyn celebration of the end of the war, *The Best Years of Our Lives* had a cast of stars: Fredric March, Myrna Loy, Teresa Wright, Dana Andrews, and Virginia Mayo. Teresa Wright was also to play the leading role in *The Bishop's Wife*, a whimsical story by Robert Nathan. Her clothes were made and the production was ready to go before the camera when it was announced that she was pregnant and that Loretta Young had been asked to play the role.

At our first meeting Loretta told me to do something to make her neck look shorter. She apparently had always disliked its length, though I thought that a considerable asset. She would have nothing to do with ruffled collars or scarves, so I had to resort to changing the proportions of the body. One cannot, however, change the proportion of one part of the body without affecting the whole figure. A sculptor made a cast of her torso and worked out a new figure. When the shoulders were raised about two inches, the line of the bosom became too low and the waist too long, so the proportions had to be adjusted. The clay model was cast to make a foam-rubber cuirass which was slit down the back to be put on and taken off like a dress. All of her costumes had to be designed with high necklines so that the edge of rubber would not show, and armholes placed very low to allow the shoulders to move fairly freely. For the sessions in which Loretta was before the camera she probably felt she had a shorter neck, though I still admired her natural one.

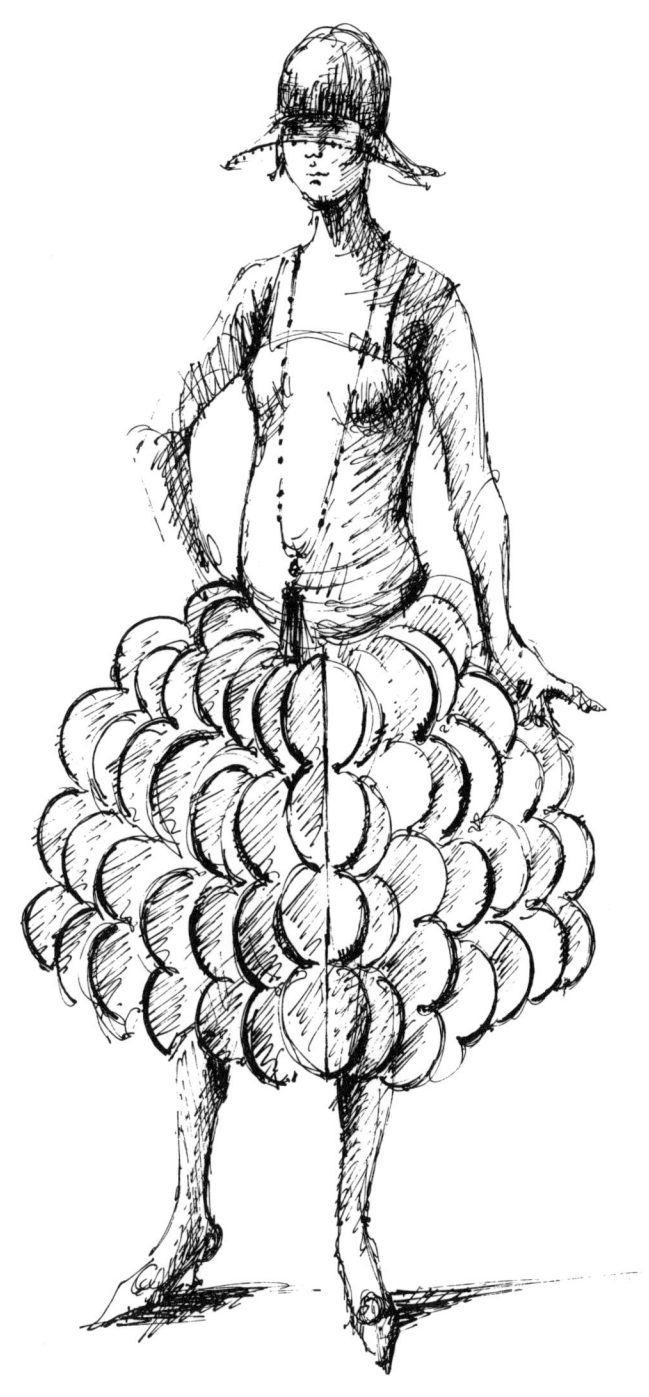

Dancer. *Billion Dollar Baby*.

At the close of the forties, with a combination of labor troubles and assets abroad frozen, Hollywood studios cut production to a minimum. The Goldwyn studio closed for a year. I worked on *Every Girl Should Be Married* for Don Hartman at RKO, a contemporary story in which Betsy Drake and Cary Grant costarred. She had a rare quality and a gift for comedy, and they were charming together on and off the screen. It was a relatively small production to design and I was able to work on the Villa-Lobos musical *Magdalena*, which was prepared and produced in Los Angeles before it opened in New York.

After *Magdalena*, from 1949 to 1959, I worked on Broadway on two straight plays and fourteen musicals, on three ballets, and on eight films in Hollywood.

Although there have been vast and various changes in the entertainment field, there is certainly a sameness in the pattern of work in any area of show business. On the other hand, there is something new each time in every production — in the fortuitous combination of the people working together on a show or film and in the requirements of each production. And as perhaps in no other business to such a degree, the unexpected constantly pops up from all directions. It is, moreover, a business in which one can never really tell while working on a production how it will turn out in its final form, or whether it will be a success or a disaster, which may partly account for the precarious dependence on luck, the inflated gambling sense, and the load of superstition prevalent in the ephemeral world of show business.

In retrospect, the musicals on Broadway that I worked on between 1949 and 1959 illustrate familiar ingredients but also some notable trends in the theater during this period. *Peepshow*, with its touch of Siam, *The King and I*, *Shangri-la*, and *Flower Drum Song* indicated a broadening interest in material about other peoples, though the stories and productions were handled from the point of view of American show business for American audiences. *A Tree Grows in Brooklyn* and *By the Beautiful Sea* — both shows with music and lyrics by Arthur Schwartz and Dorothy Fields and in both of which Shirley Booth starred — were concerned with part of the American background at the turn of the century. In *Juno*, a musical based on Sean O'Casey's *Juno and the Paycock*, Shirley co-starred with Melvyn Douglas in full Irish bloom. *Happy Hunting* was contemporary fun satire with Ethel Merman spoofing one group of the nouveau riche of America. The revival of *Of Thee I Sing* attempted to bring back political comment. *Me and Juliet* told the perennial boy-and-girl romance in a lively and tuneful show set backstage in theater. And *Candide* in 1956 and *West Side Story* in 1957, in completely different ways, set new standards on Broadway.

Dancer. *Magdalena*.

9. *An American in Paris/* "Born in a Trunk"

As a free-lance designer, I went back in 1951 to MGM and Arthur Freed to do the ballet in *An American in Paris*. The movie contained some of the best music George Gershwin composed and Ira Gershwin's inimitable lyrics. With a book by Alan Jay Lerner, Vincente Minnelli directed, and Gene Kelly and Leslie Caron starred. Gene also did the choreography. The finished movie, when it was released, ran a hundred and thirteen minutes. The ballet in it took seventeen minutes, which was considered long for a ballet in a movie.

The picture was practically completed, with only one or two scenes still to be shot, when I arrived back on the Coast. I found that they had projected a ballet in it, but no libretto had been written for it, and Freed, Vincente, and Gene had only the general idea that, since the hero was an American painter living in Paris just after the war, the ballet should have the look of French Impressionist paintings. After considerable discussion, Vincente suggested that I do the designs for the scenery and costumes and thereby indicate the story line. I was reminded of suggestions similarly expansive back in the days of the Civic, but from the start it was an exciting assignment.

I played a recording of the score over and over again until I knew the themes and movements. I made a list of the painters whose works might translate to the screen, eventually pared it down to five, visualizing how to incorporate the styles of each into the story. The movie was the love story of a young French girl and the American painter. She refuses to marry him as she feels obligated to marry an older man, her benefactor during the Nazi occupation of Paris. The ballet was the finale of the picture and had to sum up the story, with of course a happy ending.

To use various *quartiers* of Paris as backgrounds, with the settings of the five sequences to be rendered in the manner of each of the painters, I imagined the ballet as the hero's search all over the city to find the girl, who evades him till the end. This line fitted a recurring theme in Gershwin's music which reminded me of the endless walking around Paris I had done on my first visit. A small band of dancers on each of their appearances to this Gershwin theme gave unity to the ballet, and in each sequence they led to an area where the hero was looking for the girl. In uniforms derived from Parisian *pompiers* and the French Republican Guard, they marched to the music of this "walking" theme across the screen in the opening shot. Four additional characters danced by girls, whom Gene dubbed "the Furies," joined the dancers in each sequence urging the hero on in his search. They wore long tutus with intricately cut bodices and amusing headdresses; these costumes were basically the same in each sequence though in different colors. Once this integrating feature of the dancers was established, the ballet seemed to gain form. It did not take long then to write an outline with descriptions of each sequence and to indicate which painter would keynote each section.

The ballet opened in the Place de la Concorde rendered in an approximation of the style and the palette of Raoul Dufy; a mixed crowd was present, such as one sees at all hours in that part of Paris. There were dancers in smart evening clothes, visitors from all parts of the world, various Parisian types, and some characters suggested by the music, such as an African potentate.

The second section of the ballet was set in a flower market with an atmosphere suggested by the paintings of Manet. The stalls were filled with fresh flowers in the colors of his palette, and the costumes were based on figures in his paintings. The set was the simplest to design, for the flowers conveyed the idea sufficiently, although the brilliance of some of the California flowers had to be sprayed to softer tones. From the market the scene moved to a fair ground, the idea and the rendering based on a painting by Rousseau. In this sequence I was able to include the striped robe of Rousseau's *Sleeping Gypsy* for the dancers led by the heroine and ballerina of the film, Leslie Caron. For the sequence after this, I used the arches of the Paris Opera House painted on a series of "flats" (large panels) and the elaborate lamps and lamp posts around the opera house on cut-outs. To suggest the technique of Van Gogh, his broad, thickly applied brushstrokes were translated on a larger scale by the way plaster was laid on the canvas of the scenery. For both the set and the costumes the colors of his famous sunflower painting were used; the background had a pale yellow moon and stars of a creamy white in an orange sky. When I eventually saw the movie some time after it had been released, the colors in this section in that particular print of the film turned out best of the entire ballet; the range and tones of yellow, orange, green, gray, and brown came out exactly.

The sequence I enjoyed designing most was based on some of the posters and drawings of Toulouse-Lautrec. To segue from the Van Gogh section into that of the Lautrec, I drew an aimless crowd standing, as it were, in limbo on an empty canvas. As the *pompiers* danced across the screen followed by the Kelly Furies, a poster of Lautrec's Chocolat on a sandwich board on the shoulders of a dancer introduced the next scene. In a bar like one in a Lautrec drawing, Gene Kelly danced the role of Chocolat. Lautrec had known and drawn or painted many of the personalities in the theater and the music halls of his time; his style has a theatrical flair, and it was not difficult to catch something of its dramatic and decorative flavor. I had life-size figures cut out of Lucite and painted as much as possible in the Lautrec manner in the likenesses of Valentine, La Goulue, and others. The applying of the paint was deliberately sketchy to leave areas of the Lucite untouched, so that some transparency and occasional flashes of the clear Lucite added an eerie note to the scene.

When the story line for the ballet had been approved and the scenic designs accepted, Preston Ames, the art director, expertly transcribed my sketches into versions legible to the workshop for scenery. Meanwhile, I designed the three hundred costumes for the ballet, and again tried to catch the styles of the five painters. Here, again, color more than anything else was the important factor.

Place de la Concorde set and dancers in the ballet in *An American in Paris*. Courtesy Gene Kelly.

"Fury" in the ballet in *An American in Paris*.

Leslie Caron and Gene Kelly in the Toulouse Lautrec sequence of the ballet in *An American in Paris*. Courtesy Gene Kelly.

There was an air of excitement and expectancy among all of us working on the ballet which I have rarely felt in a production before or after. It was infectious, and many people on the MGM lot who had no connection with the film wandered in and out of the rehearsal hall to watch Gene work out the choreography. They stood in front of the models of the sets which Preston Ames had had made and looked long at them. They looked at photocopies of the costume sketches which, as soon as I had done them, were photographed and clipped on to a clothesline for Gene as he worked with the dancers. Even Dore Schary, then head of the studio, seemed to catch some of Freed's and our enthusiasm, for he approved the budget. When, after about ten weeks, the day of the dress rehearsal came, the way a studio could cope with the situation became evident, in great contrast to a dress rehearsal in the theater. The wardrobe department had converted a small sound stage into a huge dressing room, and here the make-up and hairdressing departments and the wardrobe men and women worked together.

The ballet had aroused interest outside the studio. Large numbers of visitors arrived on the morning of the dress rehearsal, making the occasion seem like an opening night on Broadway. Ira Gershwin, who habitually rose from his bed after noon, arrived at 9:00 A.M. on the dot.

In somewhat similar circumstances, three years after *An American in Paris*, I designed scenery and costumes for the "Born in a Trunk" number in *A Star is Born*. Harold Arlen and Ira Gershwin had done the music and lyrics for this movie, which starred Judy Garland and James Mason. Roger Edens was the composer and lyricist of "Born in a Trunk." The shooting of the picture was actually finished though not edited when it was decided to have in it the large production number. The new element was the large screen which studios were beginning to use. The drastic difference for me was in the schedule, for the number was shot at night; I found myself working on the scenery and costumes in the day and attending the shooting on the set from 7:00 in the evening till the small hours of morning.

When "Born in a Trunk" was planned, Judy had refused to work unless the number was shot at night, an ultimatum unthinkable today but which in those days a star of her standing could make and win. With her unique talents as a performer, her popularity at the box office, and with all the adulation she received from fans of all ages, Judy seemed nevertheless unable to relax and enjoy her stardom. Young and vibrant in *Meet Me in St. Louis*, when I first worked with her, she was even then tense, either way up or way down, which often resulted in a burst of tears. "Born in a Trunk" was shot at night mainly because Judy was unable to sleep and therefore willing and even eager to work at night. Fittings of her costumes had to be worked in when she was available. She always arrived with a large thermos of grapefruit juice, innocent looking enough. In the middle of one fitting I was thirsty and reached absentmindedly for the glass at hand, took a gulp, and almost keeled over from the heavy lacing of vodka.

The pattern of the night shooting indicated the almost intolerable conflict in Judy, for although she constantly complained about making movies, once the film she was making neared completion signs of panic would begin and she did not want it to end. At first, she would arrive late; sometimes she would leave before the shot was made; off and on she would not show up at all. Near the end of the shooting she insisted that a scene be shot over, then again and yet once more, till putting the number on film took as long as an average length movie. Although this exhibition smacked of gross self-indulgence, one cannot be impatient with a talent that seemed a torment at the same time that, for many years, it gave a fund of pleasure to hosts of audiences.

10. The King and I

As in *An American in Paris*, the preparation of *The King and I* in its way generated an excitement that happens once in a rare while in the theater when the people involved in a production happen to combine well and all the ingredients seem to blend smoothly, which shows in the results. Richard Rodgers and Oscar Hammerstein wrote the music and lyrics for the book by Oscar, which was based on Anna Leonowens' story of her experiences at the Siamese court in 1864. Rodgers and Hammerstein were of course the producers, assisted as usual in their productions by the indispensable Jerome Whyte. John Van Druten was the director and Jerome Robbins, the choreographer; Jo Mielziner and I designed the scenery and costumes. Gertrude Lawrence, as Anna, was the star, with Yul Brynner playing the King.

I received the script of *The King and I* while preparing the ballet in *An American in Pairs*. After the day at MGM, I started in the evening on the breakdown of the costumes and on the sketches. I borrowed a drawing board from the studio and some books of research and tried to recall some of the photographs and pictures I had examined at the time of the King of Siam's "Blue Night" in *Peepshow*. I alerted Jim Thompson that some Thai silks would be needed; and before we got into colors and details about what would be needed, he sent me copies of photographs from the Royal Archives in Bangkok. Thus for a few months I lived, as it were, in two very different countries. In the daytime I worked among things that reminded me constantly of Paris when I had been there; in the evenings I switched to a country I had never seen, which seemed exotic and remote. There was another contrast: on the one hand I was visualizing designs for film, on the other, for the stage. But I found that once I began the sketches for the theater production, I automatically returned to the approach and the drawing of sketches in the way I had been used to.

Almost my first reaction when I began to examine the research material for the costumes, was how many borrowings from Western dress there were even then in Siamese clothes. In one photograph the King wore an enormous Victorian watch and chain tucked into the pocket of his Siamese jacket. In another, he had on a full-dress uniform of a British naval commander, imaginatively embellished with curlicues of gold braid and with the broad ribbon of an order diagonally across his chest. He evidently liked hats, for in yet another photograph he was in Siamese clothes but on his head perched a Glengarry bonnet.

The Scottish element seemed to be a favorite. It was conspicuous in the dress of the amazons who guarded the women's quarters in the palace. The top part of their uniforms were fitted Siamese jackets with shoulder pieces like epaulets, only curving upwards like the corners of temple roofs; the lower part, kilts made of pleated Siamese material in plaids of brilliant colors. While the kilt, as a type of skirt, was used in ancient Egypt and would seem to have been invented as long ago as that, I could not trace the origins of the amazons' bizarre outfits; however, as the King greatly admired Queen Victoria and her far-flung empire, he may have seen some members of the Scottish regiment stationed at that time near the Siamese border and adapted what took his fancy in their uniforms for his harem guards.

In some of the photographs Jim sent me from Siam there were several of the King's wives in hoop skirts, Western bodices, and with tiny French slippers on their feet. Their hair was done in Victorian style and their jewelry was a mixture of European and Siamese pieces. The camera had caught their embarrassment as they posed to be recorded in these improvised outfits. Across almost a hundred years, their faces still expressed how uncomfortable they felt. One of the court photographs showed a fine-boned, delicate woman in a Victorian bodice above her native panung, embroidered Western stockings, and high-heeled slippers, and boldly across her bosom a wide moiré silk ribbon held in place by a jeweled order such as worn by English royalty. I adapted this lady's costume for Lady Thiang, the No. 1 wife of the King in the play. After Oscar saw the sketch he used the idea illustrated by the costume for the song "Western People Funny," which opened the second act.

The photographs of the royal children were enchanting, not only because Asian children seem generally to exude tot charm in abundance, but in these particular photographs the little boys and girls, all related through their father, wore clothes either too large or too small for them, suggesting that even among royal children clothing is handed down from the older to the younger to the smallest. All the little boys' heads were shaven except for a topknot of hair which was covered by a little tonsure "bowl." Custom decreed that these locks of hair be ceremoniously cut off during the celebration of the boy reaching manhood. The top knots covered by the "bowls," a jaunty as well as decorative note, were of course included in the costumes of the children in the play, and one was an important prop for Mrs. Anna when she sang "Getting to Know You" in the schoolroom scene.

King Mongkut in the uniform of a Naval Commander-in-Chief.

Crown Prince Chulalongkorn.

Wife of King Mongkut.

The royal children in the schoolroom. © 1956 20th Century-Fox Corp. All Rights Reserved.

The clothes indigenous to Siam in the period of the play were of a basic pattern for both men and women — skirts pleated out of yards of material tied with sashes, or panungs in which the material was ingeniously wrapped and tied in the back to form a long loin cloth rather like knickerbockers. The men sometimes wore jackets simply cut, similar to Chinese jackets, often unbuttoned with occasionally an ornate necklace on their bare chests. Some wore a variation of the long Chinese coat, heavily embroidered and in some instances lined with long-haired fur. The women wore jackets or, in the past, sometimes no tops at all; when they covered their breasts, they used a long stole pleated and wrapped around the body, leaving one shoulder bare. They wore their hair cut short, as in a crew cut, with two long strands down along their cheeks.

I gave Jim Thompson in Bangkok some idea of the colors I was planning to use in the costumes and asked him also to have woven a certain amount of the lovely yellow cloth worn by Buddhist priests and monks, for there were twelve priests in the play. Among the silks Jim eventually sent to New York was a large selection of pakomas — long and large pieces of silk, like stoles. Most of them were plaids of fresh vibrant colors; some of them had wide borders at each end into which gold or silver threads were woven; and some were made of squares of different colors.

When I showed a large number of the costume sketches to Oscar, Dick, and Van Druten, the Siamese clothes were a surprise to them, but they trustingly gave me permission to go ahead. Oscar thought that a gauze jacket in one of the King's costumes might look effeminate, though later on, when he saw the jacket on Yul Brynner, he asked for one to be made for himself.

On my way up to the office, I met Jerry Whyte coming out with Yul Brynner. It was my first meeting with Yul. Standing on the sidewalk of Madison Avenue, we talked briefly about the play when suddenly Yul asked me, "What shall I do about my hair?" He was bald with one or two strands across the top of his head and a fringe of dark hair around the back. His face, as the great number of people who saw him in the play seemed to agree, was attractive and full of vitality. On an impulse I replied "Shave it!" A look of horror crossed his face as he said, "Oh no! I can't do that. I have a dip on the top of my head. With nothing covering it I'd look dreadful." Right up to the opening in New Haven I urged him to try shaving his head, assuring him that if he was unhappy about it, it would be simple to get him a wig. I pleaded, argued, entreated, bullied. The hair got trimmed a little shorter. Finally, during the first weeks of the out-of-town run Yul shaved his head close, with not one hair in sight. With walnut juice or some concoction over his pate, which he used for make-up all over his body, he looked completely different and emerged as a glamourous personality. The effect on audiences was immediately noticeable.

During the tussle over to shave or not to shave, neither of us had an inkling of some of the consequences. For Yul's dome, hairless and gleaming, encouraged an increasing number of bald men to copy him — as if by so doing magically they too might acquire the aura and attraction he seemed to possess. What Yul's clippers achieved gave him, as it were, a logo or trademark that has taken his name. In much the same way — though of course I had nothing to do with it — Barbra Streisand's nose later on became famous, talked about, and gave reassurance to numbers of young girls with noses similar in size and shape. They copied her style of hair and dress and went around wearing their noses like badges, with a sense of belonging to an exclusive club.

I waited to design Gertrude Lawrence's costumes till we could discuss details and any preferences she had about colors — for many stars have favorite colors or certain colors they refuse to wear. Gertie had no superstitions about colors, but strong feelings about two points. From her great successes in London, where no Equity rule existed that costumes in a show had to be dry-cleaned every six weeks, she still held it would be bad luck to have her costumes dry-cleaned. She also had a notion about the letter "A" — for in every success she had been in the name of the character she had played began with an "A." As Anna in *The King and I* she was absolutely confident that the show would be a smash hit. (What a good thing for us the governess's name was not Zuleika!) No doubt this conviction buoyed her up through the pre-New York run which is always strenuous and trying in one way or another, and one can only be profoundly glad that it held for her triumphantly through a long run in her last starring role.

Yul Brynner as the King, reading the Bible, in the film *The King and I*. © 1956 20th Century-Fox Film Corp. All Rights Reserved.

When Mrs. Anna lived in Siam, the hoop skirt with long pantaloons underneath was the dominant feature of women's clothes. Gertie had seven changes of costume, each with hoops. And most of the changes had to be made quickly. Because of the hoops, the dresses could not be put on or taken off over her head. Her dresser, four wardrobe women, and the hairdresser had to be on hand for the changes. While she was on stage, two wardrobe women brought the next dress with its hoops up from the basement, laid it on the floor backstage at the point of her next entrance. The two other wardrobe women stood by at her exit point, ready when she came off stage to help her shed her costume and quickly take it away. As she stepped into the next costume, her dresser zipped it up, the hairdresser changed or rearranged her chignon, and she herself touched up her make-up. It was a tribute to that team and to Gertie herself that in one of the quick changes — between her first meeting with the King and her entrance into the schoolroom — she managed it in less than a minute and walked on stage immaculate and calm as the governess in full authority.

One costume in which Gertie charmed audiences was the ball gown which I think displayed the romantic appeal of the period. When it was being made, we did not know she would actually be dancing in it. The dress was made of a pale, dusty pink satin which, under the lights, became a subtle beige. The only decorative touch was in the silk tulle sprinkled with spangles covering the puffed sleeves at the bared shoulders, that looked like two small wings. She wore long kid gloves, and on the back of her head a snood, like a net, made of silk cord sewn with paillettes which shimmered in the light when she turned her head.

Because the cage of hoops was made of thin bamboo rings, I had tried to keep the underpinnings of all of her costumes as light in weight as possible. But when I put the half-finished gown on a figure in the workroom, the construction of the hoops showed through the lightweight material of the petticoat and the thin satin of the skirt, and the skirt fell over the hoops in a series of abrupt steps. The only way to cope with this was to have a three-tiered ruffled petticoat of a heavier material such as a stiff shantung, which however added weight to the costume. Gertie was horrified by the extra weight but, realizing that it made the gown hang properly, she accepted it.

When the song "Shall We Dance?" was put in during the Boston run, the scene became a romantic duet between Mrs. Anna and the King and included an energetic polka. Gertie found that by holding one of the hoops she could swing the entire skirt up in an arc into the air. Soon she was flinging skirt and petticoat higher and higher in big circles in the air, which thrilled the audiences. By the time the play came to New York, Gertie had so perfected her handling of the skirt that the gown became another element with her and Yul in the dance.

Anna and a pupil.

It is customary in the theater for the business manager of a production to gather bids for the making of the costumes from the firms of costume houses, and usually he assigns the job to the lowest bidder. When Brooks Costume Company offered the lowest bid in this case, I had doubts that they could meet the order satisfactorily and on time, since their workrooms were already occupied with costumes being made for a Roller Skate Follies. In fact, Brooks could not start on it for two weeks and had to hurriedly finish the sewing and fitting of costumes in the basement of the Shubert Theatre in New Haven.

As to the making of the Siamese costumes, the one and basic problem was to make garments that looked simple actually be simple to put on and take off in the theater. The panungs and the pleated skirts had to be made so that the cast did not have to drape and wrap them for each performance. The tailor and I devised a muslin foundation fitting around the hips on to which the panung or skirt was sewn. As I draped each one, the tailor firmly tacked the silk at strategic points so that the folds stayed in place. He then cut a placket down the back which was hidden by the end of the material wound around the waist but the opening of which allowed a person to put on and take off that part of the costume whole and sewn together.

Mask of Simon Legree. Courtesy Wah Chang.

Simon Legree in the ballet "The Small House of Uncle Thomas" in *The King and I*.

An amazon.

Tuptim.

The Prime Minister.

Eliza, clutching Baby George, fleeing from Simon Legree in the ballet.

In contrast to the New York workrooms, the firm in London which made the clothes for the English production had a completely different procedure. The costume house was an old one with a long and honorable record. (It no longer exists, and later at various times in London I worked with the very efficient and friendly staff of Berman's on Irving Street, off Leicester Square.) It faced Covent Garden and was close to the Drury Lane Theatre, where *The King and I* was presented. The rear windows looked out on the back of Inigo Jones' St. Paul's Church. I was surprised at the strict rule that no one except the workers were allowed in the workrooms. Thus, to begin with, I described and explained the costumes to those in charge in a small fitting room called the "Queen Victoria Room." There was another tiny room called the "Queen Alexandra Room," and these twin cubicles served as the two fitting rooms. When we had fittings of the hoop skirts on Valerie Hobson, who played Mrs. Anna, three of us could not be in the room with the hoops. The fitter and I stood in the doorway and outside, alternating to squeeze into the room to fix the costumes.

I missed not being able to have direct communication with the cutters and sewers. After I had gone through the same process with the tailor in London as with the one in New York, the panungs and the pleated skirts in muslin, draped on dummy figures, were brought down to one of the two fitting rooms. I made whatever corrections were needed. The figures were carried back up to the workrooms. This was repeated over and over again until the basic patterns were perfected. Then they were cut from the silks and the figures brought down and up over again. Nevertheless, the costumes were better made and finished than in New York.

The movie of *The King and I* made by 20th Century-Fox was predictably on a larger scale. For me, it meant a lot more costumes, and with the difference in designing for the screen, a different and a greater range of colors and color combinations. Deborah Kerr made a charming and appealing Mrs. Anna, and Yul again played the King. Rita Moreno was Tuptim and Terry Saunders Lady Thiang. Patrick Adiarte, who started out in the New York production as one of the younger children and graduated to being the Crown Prince, played the Prince again in the movie. Walter Lang was the director, Jerome Robbins, the choreographer, Leon Shamroy, the cameraman. John de Cuir was the art director and scenic designer.

There was one curious fact about the casting of the various productions of *The King and I*. When the casting call was made for the King's large family, crowds of children — Chinese, Japanese, Filipinos, and some from the Middle East — arrived. But none — except in one instance — were Siamese. The one instance was in Hollywood, when Siamese triplets turned up among the children with their parents clamoring to be in the film. About six years old, the three were identical — silent and standing apart from the other children. One could not tell one from the others. Walter Lang grabbed my arm and exclaimed, "Wouldn't you know! I thought it was going to be difficult to find a pair of Asian twins. Here we have triplets. But if we use them, everyone will say 'Isn't that just like Hollywood, always exaggerating'!"

11. *Porgy and Bess/Can-Can/* Khrushchev visits 20th Century-Fox

The big screen once conspicuous for its size is now taken for granted. Landscapes and vistas on it are generally superb. Interiors and close-ups on the large screen, however, often point up the problems of awkward proportions and the vast expanse that has to be composed. But when many films look so good on the large screen, it is footling to carp at the bigness or to wonder, given the same quality of presentation — as for instance, in Ingmar Bergman's *Cries and Whispers* — whether the size of the screen matters.

The big screen was certainly an advantage in Sam Goldwyn's productions of *Guys and Dolls* and *Porgy and Bess.* Both pictures also gained a great deal from technical improvements rapidly being made in quality of film, color processing, and sound reproduction.

Behind the Goldwynisms such as "Include me out," "I want a close-up with feet," which had their peculiar wit, Sam Goldwyn had a sure instinct that seemed most of the time to hit the mark in every department of movie making. In *Guys and Dolls,* the script called for a wedding dress for Jean Simmons — a simple outfit, appearing as it did after the Salvation Army uniform worn through most of the picture. The sketch was approved by Sam and the director, Joe Mankiewicz. Then one day, before the dress was put into work, as Sam and I were walking down the midway, he suddenly grabbed my arm and said, "How about the uniform and holding the bouquet instead of the wedding dress?" Ordinarily I would have put such a query down to his shrewd budget-paring, but in this instance he was absolutely right. The incident, brief and beyond the film of no consequence, won me over.

In the six movies I worked on for Sam Goldwyn, we bickered and disputed; it was sometimes rough going, but basically — particularly through the last two productions — he treated me as a colleague and I was one among his host of admirers. There were also many funny moments, as when Sam, reviewing the line-up of the show girls in a number, put his hands on what he thought was too much padding of a bosom and turned to me to make the correction. She happened to be the only one who had no padding on at all.

Anyone working at the Goldwyn studio could not be unaware of Mrs. Goldwyn, unobtrusive, indispensable to Sam in the office and on the lot, and unfaltering moral support for all of us. She was a reassuring presence, especially in the preparation of the production of *Porgy and Bess.*

Long before the film, *Porgy and Bess* was first a book by Du Bose Heyward, then a play. In 1935 it appeared on Broadway as George Gershwin's "American folk opera" with libretto and lyrics by Heyward and Ira Gershwin. As with *Candide* years later, the critics could not decide whether to treat the Theatre Guild production as opera, operetta, or musical. Revived in 1940 by Cheryl Crawford, with significant changes of recitatives into speeches, it was a great success, eventually applauded in cities all over the world.

As a film, it was a large and complicated project in which an unusually fine coordination was needed between story, performance, and music. There were obstacles from the start. When Sam was mulling over the casting, he asked Leontyne Price to sing — and only to sing — the role of Bess, which would be dubbed in later. Understandably, he got the curt rejoinder, "No body, no voice."

From the beginning there was malaise among the cast, which was a talented and distinguished group headed by Sidney Poitier, Dorothy Dandridge, Sammy Davis Jr., Pearl Bailey, Brock Peters, and Diahann Carroll. Torn between being in an important production with high salaries and what they construed as Uncle Tomism in the story, their uneasiness broke out in many ways, at one point in refusing to work. Concentrated on the costumes, I had at first only a hint of the dissension when Pearl Bailey, at a fitting, refused to wear a bandanna. Since the character she played probably did not wear one all the time, I let it go.

I was well aware that the bandanna had become a detested emblem among blacks, but in many of the photographs taken in Charleston in 1911, the locale and the period of the story, the bandanna tied around the head was a common feature of the women's clothes. The principals and the women singers in the picture who were to wear them accepted the bandanna as part of the costume. When, however, they lined up for the first costume review before the final dress parade, Pearl caused havoc by screaming, "No one is going to wear a bandanna in any picture I'm in!" Slowly, one by one, those wearing bandannas removed the offending item. A white journalist, interviewing Pearl during a nightclub engagement before the film started, had asked her why she had accepted the role in the movie. He had heard that all black performers felt strongly that the film should not be made. Mischievously he asked if she was going to wear one of those Aunt Jemima bandannas, at which she apparently hit the roof and swore she would not. At the costume review, a discussion somewhat like an international conference ensued, and a compromise was reached whereby only a few of the women at a time would wear bandannas — and I might add, nothing like Aunt Jemima's but in rather lovely muted colors. Like the proverbial tempest in a teacup, the incident now seems ridiculous, particularly since shortly afterwards many black women took to wearing bandannas as symbols of what they were fighting about.

The day set for a run-through of the dance number of Sportin' Life happened to be Yom Kippur. Everyone concerned was present except Sammy Davis, who played Sportin' Life. When Goldwyn was informed that, as a convert to Judaism, Sammy would not be coming to the rehearsal hall till after sundown, he was enraged. Everything had to be put off to start at the end of the working day. The delay and prospects of overtime costs left him fuming, "I don't need *him* to show me how to be a good Jew!"

A real disaster occurred after we had been preparing for the film about four months, when the set and the costumes were destroyed by fire. Frances Goldwyn telephoned me at 6:00 A.M. of the day on which the first complete rehearsal before the camera had been scheduled. Through the fog of sleep — and with some surprise at the hour — I recognized her voice, as always calm and soothing, though with a distinct note of warning. She was telling me, in substance, first to keep cool, then about the fire on the lot and on the main sound stage where we were all to have gathered at 9:00 A.M. The fire had started before dawn and by the time I got to the studio after the call, it was raging. The one large set Oliver Smith had designed for Catfish Row was completely demolished. So were the costumes of the principals and of some of the cast, as well as sketches which a wardrobe girl had taken to the set so they would be available during the rehearsal and costume tests. Most of us present thought the production would be cancelled. But the set was rebuilt, the costumes were made again, and production resumed.

In retrospect, *Porgy and Bess* was one of the most interesting pictures for which I designed costumes. I had to hew a very close line so that they would look neither too realistic nor too theatrical. A major problem was to age the costumes properly. The ageing methods used on costumes generally work adequately for a few outfits in a production, but for a whole company would look artificial. The clothes in the film were presumably the only ones that the characters possessed, perhaps hand-me-downs in the first place, and were supposed to have been worn day in and day out for years. There were a great number of these costumes, and they were worn by the large cast through the whole picture. Luckily I found a cache of clothes made around the turn of the century. The time between then and 1911 and the circumstances of the story made the general silhouette and lines acceptable. I had them bleached, then dyed in soft subdued tones of a controlled color scheme. With a few changes in line and proportions, the clothes were assigned to the various characters to make the most of the relationships in this palette.

Shortly after *Porgy and Bess*, I worked at 20th Century-Fox on *Can-Can*, another musical with late-nineteenth-century costumes. The film was directed by Walter Lang and contained a galaxy of stars: Shirley MacLaine, Frank Sinatra, Maurice Chevalier, Juliet Prowse, and Louis Jourdain. There was an "Adam and Eve" fantasy ballet choreographed by Hermes Pan. Except for Adam and Eve, the twenty-five dancers represented animals, birds, and other inhabitants of Eden — among them a lion as a maharajah, and the frog, a footman — with heads identifying the species. The ballet was keyed in beige and black with touches of color in the clothes. The heads of the animals, birds, and insects were executed by Wah Chang, a sculptor with whom I worked on several pictures, whose talents included a wonderful sense of fantasy and a sense of humor which added greatly to this ballet.

Bess in the film *Porgy and Bess*.

Sportin' Life. *Porgy and Bess.*

Turkey in "Adam and Eve" ballet in the film *Can-Can*.

Dragonfly in "Adam and Eve" ballet.

Tiger in "Adam and Eve" ballet.

Can-Can was in production over ten years ago. By chance it added a historical footnote because Khrushchev visited on the set. For days before the entourage arrived, American and Russian secret-service men clutching Geiger counters prowled around the studio, pored over every inch of the sound stage where carpenters had built a platform from which the party was to watch a run-through of a scene. Everyone working on the film was screened — in the secret-service sense, not the movie term — and given identity badges in order that we could continue working on the lot during those days.

Khrushchev and his party, coming direct from the airport, arrived in time for lunch. It happened to be a very hot day, and although the California sun was at its brightest, the smog smothered the city and increased the discomfort of the heat. The Russians, their faces flushed and streaked with perspiration, wore heavy woolen clothing. Ushered immediately to the commissary, they were palpably relieved to enter the air-conditioned hall where Spyros Skouras and his entourage awaited them. Once the Russian photographers spotted the array of Hollywood stars invited to the lunch, they went berserk, snapping pictures of one, then the next, and the next. Elizabeth Taylor, insouciant, wearing a large sable hat, a dress with a diving neckline, and dripping diamond earrings, was the focus of the Russian photographers' attention. Their crowding around the stars' tables left Khrushchev and Skouras in a sort of splendid isolation at their table on the dais. It must have been a novel experience for Khrushchev at that moment to have Russians turn their backs on him and forget he was in the room.

During the lunch Mrs. Khrushchev sent her husband a note. It apparently notified him their trip to Disneyland afterwards had been canceled because it presented insurmountable problems in guarding the Russian visitors. For the Russian party, it was to have been the high point of their Hollywood trip. Mrs. Khrushchev made no bones about her displeasure. Her husband had already been displeased by remarks in a speech by Mr. Skouras. So there was a noticeable drop in cordiality at their tables, not helpful to the entertainment they were to see on the set after lunch.

With a touch of gaucheness, the studio chose to show the can-can number to the Russian visitors. The girls, led by Shirley MacLaine, went into the dance in high gear, flaunting much leg in a whirl of petticoats. Shirley had spent so much time memorizing a speech of welcome in Russian that she had not had much time for rehearsing and was often out of step with the other dancers. Immediately after the strenuous dance, she launched into the speech. Khrushchev showed his mounting rage, which was reflected in Mrs. Khrushchev's green pin-point eyes. Shaking hands rather abruptly all around, they quickly left the set.

The Khrushchevs with Spyros Skouras on the *Can-Can* set. N.R. Farbman/*Time-Life* Picture Agency. © Time Inc.

12. West Side Story/Candide

West Side Story was produced on Broadway in 1957 and as a film in 1961. When it appeared on Broadway, it was one of the few musicals with a serious contemporary story in that it dealt with the rivalry between two teen-age gangs on the streets of New York. It was loosely based on *Romeo and Juliet*. For years Jerome Robbins had had in mind a modern version with the two feuding families changed to Jewish and Italian groups. Arthur Laurents, who wrote the book for the production, shifted the identity of the teen-age gangs, making one Puerto Rican and the other, a group of other young Americans. The combination of idea, story, Jerry's direction and choreography, with the score by Leonard Bernstein and lyrics by Stephen Sondheim, introduced a fresh note in musical theater. Oliver Smith and I designed the scenery and costumes for the stage production. On the film Boris Levin was the art director and scenic designer.

In the costumes for both stage and screen versions of *West Side Story* exaggeration and fantasy had no place, and literalness would not have helped visually. I relied on color to contrast the two gangs, with touches in their outfits that were taken from Renaissance clothes. In the fifties, the teen-age boys one saw on the streets of New York had arrived at a uniform of their own — not yet taken up as fashionable by men and women — consisting of blue jeans or chinos, T-shirts, windbreakers, and sneakers. It was of course an outfit economical and comfortable. For the Sharks, the Puerto Rican gang, I used sharp purple, pink-violet, blood red, and black; for the Jets, the other gang, I chose muted indigo blues, musty yellows, and ochre. The colors seemed to suit their physical appearance; moreover, even though in the story the Puerto Ricans were the weaker gang and on the defensive, their outfits gave them an aggressive quality.

The windbreaker now seems so much a part of the contemporary scene that one forgets it is a jacket of considerable vintage, traceable to the shepherd's coat, which was a basic garment centuries ago. It is an example of articles of clothing originally made to be functional, acquiring a classic beauty, and from time to time copied and adapted by fashion and thus never out of date. The modern windbreaker with a hood, particularly when worn with tight-fitting jeans, has a silhouette and line resembling that of figures in Florentine Renaissance paintings. Those worn by the gangs in *West Side Story* were varied by using one color in front, another in the back, with a sharp contrast in the color of the sleeves. The seams of the jackets were bound with narrow satin edging, again in contrasting color, so that as the dancers moved, their jackets seemed faceted in color. The T-shirt, which up to the fifties was worn solely as underwear, when dyed, gave the dancers the air of trapezists.

The girls in the play wore clothes that were less uniform and that could be given more theatricality. Again color was important. The Puerto Rican girls were naturally more exotic looking than the Jet gang's girls — one of whom dressed like the boys. The one article of clothing of ethnic character the Puerto Rican girls wore was the rebozo, the long woolen stole with fringed ends worn around the shoulders and sometimes also over the head in Mexico and the Caribbean area. In the last scene, when the hero was shot, the rebozos over the girls' heads made them look like traditional figures of mourning.

In contrast to *West Side Story*, *Candide*, produced in 1956, required hundreds of costumes and in great variety. Since it was a story of Everyman, costumes of three centuries were designed: Westphalian and Portuguese peasant clothes of the seventeenth century, Italian costumes and German uniforms of the eighteenth, French ball gowns, Spanish clothes, and uniforms of the nineteenth. There were also ecclesiastical robes and Turkish and South American Indian costumes. With a book by Lillian Hellman, another superb score by Leonard Bernstein, lyrics by Richard Wilbur and others, it was a small-scale opera calling for well-trained singers. Ethel Linder Reiner had great courage — and enormous expense — in bringing the production to Broadway. Robert Rounseville, Barbara Cook, Max Adrian, and Irra Petina headed the cast. They were magnificent in difficult parts with exacting demands in singing. On opening night Barbara Cook's "Jewel Song" was a peak in voice and performance that is still thrilling to recall.

As to the making of the costumes, *Candide* was not only a large and varied production to design, it was also the only time I thought a particular costume house in New York could turn out the wide range and number of costumes with style. I asked the producer to let Karinska execute the costumes; although it meant higher costs, the producer assigned the job to her. I do not think it was a mistake, but certainly we had trouble from the start. For, without the producer or I knowing till it was too late, Karinska took on also the costumes for an opera. Consequently, the *Candide* costumes did not arrive on time or properly finished for the dress rehearsal or the first night in Boston. It was a hair-raising experience and, as the designer, I naturally had to take the blame. It was nevertheless not as bad as what happened even before the making of the costumes started. If one speaks in terms of "hair-raising," it is a wonder some of us were not bald by the time *Candide* opened out of town.

Maria in the mock-wedding scene, *West Side Story.*

Boys of the Jets gang, *West Side Story.*

Boys of the Sharks gang, *West Side Story.*

Anita in the Gym Dance number, *West Side Story.*

Girls in the Gym Dance number, *West Side Story*.

Two kings in a transition scene, *Candide*.

Three women in the "Lisbon earthquake" scene, *Candide*.

When Karinska was given the job of executing the costumes, I handed her at the end of the week a portfolio of about two hundred and fifty costume sketches, with memos on most of them pertaining to materials, colors, and other details, for her to look over during the weekend. We made a date to meet on the Monday to discuss the costumes and to start choosing materials. She turned up at my apartment on Sunday morning. Taking one look at her face, and hearing at the same time that she had just lit a candle at the church on the corner, I sensed disaster. I quickly led her to a chair and gave her a stiff brandy. As she revealed the sad tidings, it was necessary to pour her more support, for she had left the portfolio of sketches in a taxi. They were lost. She could not remember whether it had been a yellow cab, a green one, or another kind. I was stunned and for some minutes speechless. Then, as I started to ask her if she had telephoned the Lost and Found Departments of the cab companies, she suddenly pulled handkerchiefs out of her handbag and the scarf from around her neck and began to tie them on the legs of chairs and tables. Seeing her at this, I had a fleeting thought that one of us must be going mad. However, she in turn started to reassure me by explaining that that was what they used to do in Russia, at the same time fervently praying, to find something lost or mislaid. Absurd or not, in a few days, during which frantic efforts were made to trace the sketches, the portfolio was retrieved.

Post-mortems on shows are generally useless. One cannot, however, help wondering about *Candide*, which was quite rapturously applauded by audiences but by no means had a long run. It had all the elements of a potentially big success: a dramatic script, lyrics with wit, an enchanting score, good singers, visual excitement. But the staging was cumbersome. Tyrone Guthrie, the director, had gained a reputation with operas and with classics in the theater, but had never tackled a musical. At the start, in fact, he declared a choreographer was unnecessary and used a friend who had helped him with crowd scenes in other productions to improvise the dances. Only at the last minute did he accept Anna Sokolow to try and give the dances form and the professional zip which was needed. In any case, since the original production, the presentation of *Candide* on the concert stage and in other forms suggests that, like Voltaire's classic, it contains the ingredients that continue to entertain and to please.

13. *Cleopatra*

Walter Wanger's office at 20th Century-Fox was across the hall from mine while I was working on *Can-Can*, and he used to drop in to chat and look at the costume sketches. One day he asked me to lunch in the commissary with Johnny de Cuir, whom we found waiting there with a large portfolio of sketches beside him. The sketches were of settings for a film about Cleopatra which Walter was planning. It was projected as a small, intimate picture to be made on the studio lot, with a small budget. Walter said he would like a star but was quite ready to search for a new personality for the part. When he asked me to design the costumes for the picture, I remember I burst out laughing and said that any film about Cleopatra could hardly avoid looking like a production of *Aida*. Walter and Johnny were not amused, nor did they like my suggestion that perhaps the way to design it would be to camp it, using the Victorian painters' interpretations of Romans and Egyptians.

I did not hear anything more about this project for over a year. Meanwhile the production had magnified. Elizabeth Taylor was playing Cleopatra, there was an international supporting cast, and the film was being made in London. The weather had not been propitious. The bared arms and knees of the extras as Roman soldiers were visibly blue from cold in some scenes already shot; chills and illness were rife in the company. Elizabeth caught pneumonia and was hospitalized. The studio shelved the small amount of film that had been shot and closed down the production. Joseph Mankiewicz was called in to write a new script and to direct the picture. I was finishing my work on the film of *West Side Story* when I heard from Walter on his return from London. He asked me to design the costumes for Elizabeth in *Cleopatra*.

Circumstances during the filming of *Cleopatra*, exaggerated and over publicized, do not need to be warmed up again. A few situations and some account of the costumes do, however, have a place in these pages.

With Walter and Joe I looked at the costume tests of Elizabeth and some of the scenes that had been filmed in London. I realized why the studio and Walter had decided to start over again and with a fresh script. I was assured freedom in designing Cleopatra's clothes, but it was obvious that a direction had already been set. Costumes for some of the principals and the supporting cast, already made, had to serve in the new production. Settings had been decided on. They followed the stereotyped view of Egypt long before Cleopatra was born.

As to Cleopatra's clothes, documentation of what was worn in Egypt in the first century B.C. is sparse. The bas-relief at Denderah purporting to represent Cleopatra shows the elaborate crown and collar of an Egyptian goddess, typical of the divinities in the frescoes in ancient tombs. Since at that later date she was probably included in the pantheon, and so garbed, it did not mean that during her life she dressed like that, except for sacred ceremonial occasions. The few photographs I found of fragments of sculpture and coins that have occasionally been very tentatively linked to Cleopatra suggest only that she was plump, had a large nose, and that her hair was dressed much like any Roman matron of her times. The trade relations between the two countries must have carried continuous mutual influences. Cleopatra, as a Macedonian, as a ruler, and as a woman, was undoubtedly astute and surely delighted in anything novel from Rome or ports on the trade routes to add to her personal adornment. I was lucky to find a photograph of a small headless statue in the Cairo Museum, whose dress gave me the clue to designing Cleopatra's costumes. The tight-fitting bodice showed fine lines of trapunto or, as it is now more commonly called, quilting, one of the oldest forms of decoration.

The script called for sixty changes of costume for Cleopatra, from a girl of seventeen to a woman of thirty-seven. One tends to think of Cleopatra as looking the same through her relatively short life, but of course the maturing had to be indicated. I found this was easiest to handle by dividing the costumes into three groups, and by the use of various styles of wigs which were made expertly by Stanley Hall in London. All the ceremonial costumes were based on ancient Egyptian tomb paintings; the second group were clothes such as Roman women of the upper classes might have worn; and the last group made use of one of the oldest garments, the djellabah.

The materials used in Egypt and Rome in the first century B.C. were similar in look and drape to some that are used today. Although jersey is a modern fabric, when it is softly pleated it hangs like the material we see on Roman statues. As a silk jersey drapes wonderfully well, many of Cleopatra's costumes were made of it. For others, I used fine wool, sheer gauzes, and thin cottons. I depended on heavy embroidery on the ceremonial robes.

During the filming and in the promotion of the picture much was made of the gold ceremonial costume that Cleopatra wore at her entrance into Rome. The cost of making the complete costume — about two thousand dollars — was blown up by publicity to triple and quadruple that sum. What was really remarkable was the work done on it with extraordinary patience and skill by Hollywood seamstresses and embroiderers. The dress was made of gold lamé, with a shell pattern embroidered with gold bullion. For the wings of Isis which went with it, I drew the pattern in exact size. Their foundation was a coarse net, on which were appliquéd pieces of thin gold kid cut in the form of stylized feathers. The headdress was topped by a crown, based on the one on the bas-relief at Denderah, formed by a circle of cobras and the sun disk and the two feathers associated with the goddess Isis. Wah Chang executed the elaborate crown out of papier-mâché.

Walter, as the producer, gallantly entertained socialites and celebrities and visiting movie stars in the Cinecittà commissary. One day, lunching the Baroness de Rothschild, he was in full steam about the gold costume. At a neighboring table I heard him announce "seven thousand dollars!" She, hardly turning her head, remarked that for that sum she could not even get a raincoat at Balenciaga.

For all the glitter and gold of the ceremonial costume, I enjoyed most designing the djellabahs. I liked working out their decoration, using hieroglyphs or Egyptian symbols such as the eye of Horus, the ankh, the *djed*-pillar.

Most of the major museums in America and in Europe have collections of ancient Egyptian and Roman jewelry. As the pieces are carefully dated or attributed to definite periods, I had many actual designs to draw on. Two of the necklaces for Cleopatra came out very well: one was made of two-inch scarabs of emerald green glass flecked with gold and linked by rings; and the other, of simulated gold using a bee motif.

When I started to design Elizabeth's costumes, there was neither a finished script nor a shooting schedule. I had a rough breakdown of the scenes in which she appeared, by which to figure out what would be needed and which scenes were likely to be shot first. Since the ceremonial costumes were the most complicated to make and would need more time, I started them in Hollywood and also put into work there others, totaling sixteen. The rest of her costumes were made at the same costume house in Rome where additional costumes were being made for the new cast and for the crowd scenes. The two other designers on the film and I were lucky to have Courtney Haslam of 20th Century-Fox in Rome for the first few weeks to organize and handle the business details.

As winter crept in, I could understand why the workers at the costume house wore heavy sweaters and high boots — later taken up as fashionable. Traversing the marble floors in the old palazzo where the costumes were made was like walking on ice cubes. In the workroom there was one tiny fireplace which gave out a great deal of smoke but barely a whiff of heat. However, as with most of the craftsmen I worked with in Rome, the workers were extraordinarily inventive and skillful.

I had an interpreter, Irina Wassilichikov, gifted in half a dozen languages, who helped me communicate with the fitters and sewers. Interpreters were necessary in every department. On the set, an Italian assistant director relayed Joe's directions to the crowds in a routine similar to the continuous translation at U.N. meetings. Irina and I functioned on a double work day, for the filming at Cinecittà was on a schedule of American working hours and including Saturdays, but the costume house and Roman shops kept Roman hours with the siesta from one to four inviolable.

One of Cleopatra's costumes using trapunto. © 1963 20th Century-Fox Productions, Ltd.

Headless statue in the Cairo Museum, showing trapunto or quilting.

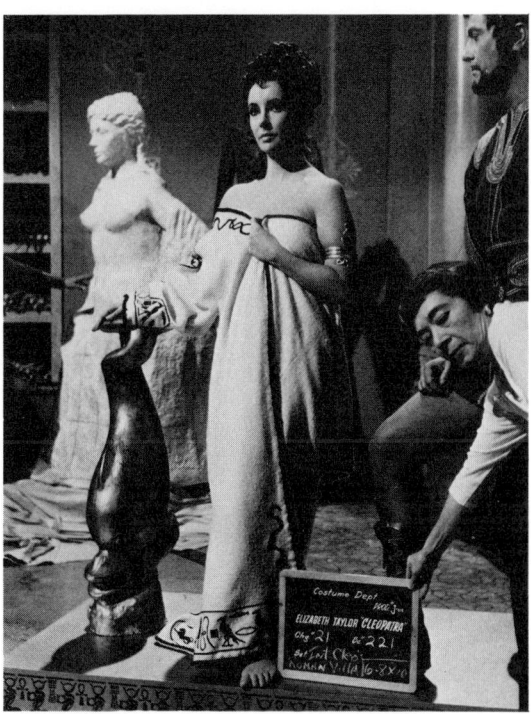

Robe in scene posing for a sculptor, with Cleopatra's name in hieroglyphs applied as decoration of border. © 1963 20th Century-Fox Productions, Ltd.

One of Cleopatra's costumes in "Roman Villa" section of the film. © 1963 20th Century-Fox Productions, Ltd.

Costume in the Farewell Scene with Caesar. © 1963 20th Century-Fox Productions, Ltd.

Costume test still: a headdress and jewelry including the scarab necklace. © 1963 20th Century-Fox Productions, Ltd.

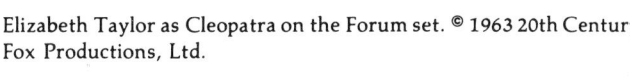

Elizabeth Taylor as Cleopatra on the Forum set. © 1963 20th Century-Fox Productions, Ltd.

Figure on bas-relief at Denderah.

The logistics of a large production on location abroad are extremely complex. It was a formidable task for those in charge. The American company numbered over a hundred, including technicians and working crews; the Italians and Europeans in the company, not counting the actors and actresses and extras, more than doubled the number.

To mention the size of the production is to repeat the most conspicuous and most publicized fact about it. Equally obvious, the Romans made the most of it in every profitable way. In addition, the picture drew hordes of tourists. The concierge at the Eden Hotel was quite breathless with excitement, breaking his usual imperturbable calm, when he spoke of the number of visitors who chose to look at the Forum set instead of the historical ruins of the original. Besides, the elephants for Cleopatra's procession into Rome were housed on a back lot at Cinecittà, throwing in, as it were, a visit to a zoo.

I had met Elizabeth at Jeannie Simmons' and the Ira Gershwins' homes, but when the preparation for *Cleopatra* started, Hollywood protocol evidently dictated that we should be introduced formally. Walter, who rather enjoyed that sort of thing, took me to meet Elizabeth. During *Cleopatra* I came to like her enormously, admiring qualities that are obscured by the blatant publicity that seems invariably to surround her. I was not awed by her, for when one spends a lot of time in fitting rooms with stars, men and women, they are as anyone else in underwear at fittings, far from perfect in proportions and in most instances with problems which have to be taken into account in designing their clothes. At that time Elizabeth's face, with her extraordinary violet eyes, was probably one of the loveliest in the world. For a designer, however, she was five feet two and had difficult proportions: high waist, large bosom, short arms, no behind, but wide hips. Her personal taste in clothes, as she herself remarked, often turned out like a chorus girl's.

In the midst of the designing and making of Elizabeth's costumes, I was summoned to the projection room where Walter and Joe were looking at the costume tests of Rex Harrison, who was about to go before the camera in his role of Julius Caesar. The tests were run again to loud complaints from both of them about how Rex looked in his costumes. The costumes were faithful reproductions of what was worn by one of high rank in Rome in 52 B.C., but as Rex himself remarked later, they made him "look like an old Charlie." Without the fine tailoring of Savile Row, Rex's figure was not impressive. The Roman costumes with tunics and short sleeves exposed the weak points: narrow shoulders, long thin arms, spindly legs. Whether Caesar had an imposing figure or not may perhaps concern historians, but for an actor appearing as Caesar on the big screen it would have been disastrous to exhibit the defects. "Look," Joe said, "you've got to help us out. Rex can't look like that. Do something!" In the doing I learned an interesting historical footnote.

I found in Suetonius a description of Caesar's taste in clothes. "His dress was, it seems, unusual: he had added wrist-length sleeves with fringes to his purple-striped senatorial tunic, and the belt which he wore over it was never tightly fastened — hence Sulla's warning to the aristocratic party: 'Beware of that boy with the loose clothes!'"(Reprinted from *Suetonius:The Twelve Caesars* translated by Robert Graves by permission of Robert Graves.) Evidently Caesar wore what he pleased; certainly long sleeves with fringes were not generally worn in his day.

I remembered the foam rubber torso I had had made for Loretta Young and now used the idea for Rex. A sculptor made a cast of the torso, then broadened the shoulders and increased the girth; he also made some "symmetricals" to be added to the thighs and calves. These were cast in foam rubber which a seamstress in the workrooms chose, with a fine Roman touch, to cover with bright pink silk. All of this gave Rex "build" and was flexible enough for freedom of movement. Instead of the short tunic with pleated skirt generally worn under the military cuirass, I designed a leather jerkin with long sleeves. The greaves worn over the shins partly covered leather breeches. A cuirass worn by a military commander would have been elaborately decorated, but for Rex I designed instead one of dark polished leather unadorned except for the usual sculptured suggestion of a man's torso. Over his shoulders he wore a heavy red woolen cloak. Although this description of the outfit with its foundation may make it seem complicated, visually it was simple and made him look quite startlingly dramatic. I used the same license in his other costumes, stripping them to the basic form and using practically no decoration. His senatorial robe was pleated and reached to the ground; the toga worn over it added bulk to the silhouette. There was only one snag — in his final scene, when the conspirators converged on him at the foot of Pompey's statue. They flourished rubber daggers filled with red fluid for the

Antony, Caesar, and Augustus on the Senate steps awaiting Cleopatra's formal entrance into Rome. © 1963 20th Century-Fox Productions, Ltd.

murderous deed, but striking Rex's foam-rubber padding, the daggers bounced off. The problem was solved, and with Caesar's death, Rex completed an impressive, and perhaps the best, performance in the film.

The first scene shot in Rome — Cleopatra's entrance into the Forum of the ancient city — not only required the largest number of extras in the picture, but illustrates the bad luck with weather that was unpredictable and so costly. This scene was scheduled first to use the Forum set immediately (in August, when presumably the weather would be sunny and clear) and also to get the large crowd scene finished at the beginning. Four thousand extras were crowded on the set; the star's trailers were lined up on the side along with a Red Cross wagon. The cameras were on their booms, the phalanx of reflectors was set up, and all the crews were standing by. The procession preceding Cleopatra, as it approached the Senate steps, had warriors, musicians, slaves, and dancing girls — the whole caboodle outdoing even the *Aida* effects I had joked about to Walter. About a quarter of the scene was shot, when suddenly the weather changed from sunlight to clouds to heavy rain. The shooting stopped. The filming continued with indoor scenes on the sound stages. The torrential rains continued, which every Roman around, half in condolence, half in glee, and with the inevitable charming gestures, assured us was very unusual. It was not till almost nine months later that the rest of the procession scene could be shot.

In the interim, during the shooting of indoor scenes, the Taylor-Burton romance caused almost as much havoc with the schedule as the weather had on the Forum set. It apparently started in the scene in Cleopatra's villa in Rome. Elizabeth was wearing a softly pleated silk jersey costume of primrose yellow. Later on, during Richard's tour in *Hamlet* before coming to New York, she telephoned and asked me to design her wedding dress. I designed the modern dress for her in the same yellow. Yes, we show-folk are on occasion awash with sentiment.

A word might be added about Cleopatra and the asp, not only because the actual event is legendary, but because the shooting of the scene illustrates the lengths to which a studio felt it had to go to meet the demands of realism in movies. It also points the rather devastating contrast between, on the one hand, the little asp and a few figs, and on the other, the elaborate preparations for the scene. A real asp was used, with its keeper protectively garbed and armed with a long pair of tongs. Medical personnel and other precautions were required in case the snake slithered out of control. Because of the unavoidable changes in the shooting schedule, figs were not in season in Italy at the time the scene was shot and a basketful had to be flown in from Libya. On the set, when the little black asp was let out of its box for the shot of it emerging from the basket of figs, it found itself surrounded by the crews and the bright lights and was apparently terrified. Its keeper prodded and poked, but it refused to budge. Finally persuaded to move, it was caught by the camera as it slid down the steps of the dais and headed for shelter at the base of a tall stand holding a brazier near the catafalque.

Between the first attempt to shoot the Forum scene and the last scene shot in Ischia there were numerous and incredibly frustrating delays. At long last, however, the company left for Ischia for the remaining outdoor scenes of

Cleopatra's barge. A tiny port on the island, where little had to be done architecturally for background, served as the ancient city of Tarsus where Cleopatra and Antony had their historic confrontation. The interior scenes on board the barge had already been shot in Rome. The barge itself had been built on the hull of an old coal carrier. It was safe enough in the small port at Ischia but too frail for any other and larger port in that part of the Mediterranean.

Historically, Cleopatra's barge is famous, among other things, for having a female crew. In 1962, this fact only added to the accumulated troubles of the production. A week before the company left for Ischia someone in the wardrobe department reported that no costumes existed for Cleopatra's crew. The girls, moreover, were to be chosen at Ischia and, if necessary, in Naples. The two other designers on the film, not knowing about these costumes, had finished their work and returned to Hollywood. I was again asked, with some urgency, to "do something."

Having searched for items needed for Elizabeth's costumes, I had come to know parts of Rome well, especially some small supply shops on side streets. I bought the entire stock of artificial flowers in a small millinery supply shop and had the wardrobe women twist them into wreaths for the girls' heads. Some ersatz chiffon was dyed into various gay colors, two lengths for each girl to be pinned at the shoulders, draped, and tied with silk cords around the waist. The total cost of the materials for the seventy-five girls equaled the complete costumes of two spear carriers.

No sooner had we coped with this problem, however, when, two days before leaving for Ischia, word came that a crew of Neapolitan sailors had to handle the sailing of the barge. The men would be seen only in a long shot but had to be dressed somewhat similarly to the girl crew. Many yards of cheesecloth were quickly dyed pale blue, and we made up some more wreaths. When I draped those "costumes," they looked hilariously silly and the general laughter verged on hysteria when the sailors refused to take off their wristwatches. Hilyard Brown, who had found the coal carrier and supervised the building of the barge, was on board. He had to wear the cheesecloth and a wreath, and held more flowers to hide the walkie-talkie through which he issued orders to the boat pulling the barge. Thus the making of *Cleopatra* ended, not with a bang, by no means with a whimper, but in a mad scramble.

14. Elizabeth/Stardom/Barbra

During the production of *Cleopatra* and later in *The Sandpiper, Who's Afraid of Virginia Woolf?* and *The Taming of the Shrew,* in all four of which Elizabeth costarred with Richard Burton, I worked and shared the intimacy peculiar to movie making with them. It was an experience off and on of "glamour" past and present style. At times, it was like visiting the Hollywood of the magazines. Often, the more human side showed. Frequently, one was only too conscious of the hard facts of stardom. To weather them Elizabeth evidently has the guts and the stamina.

The Sandpiper was an inane story which the Burtons bore stoically. About one third of it was made in Big Sur, California, the locale of the film in which Elizabeth played a hippie painter and Richard a clergyman-schoolmaster. Most of the picture was filmed in Paris, which meant reproducing California interiors on the sound stages at the Billancourt studios. It also required shipping twenty-four sandpipers from the Big Sur beach along with the equipment, props, furniture, and costumes.

Native to the West Coast, these perky little birds with long thin legs are extremely delicate. They are invisibly protected by state laws. As the title of the film suggests, with symbolic hokum, a live sandpiper, frail and vulnerable, was essential to the story and indeed had an important scene with the star. But to transport one — not to mention two dozen — MGM and the producer had to sign papers binding them to return the sandpipers to the beach of Big Sur. The birds had two caretakers and special food and water. Nine died in Paris. One, which was in the scene with Elizabeth, was supposed to fly across the room on to her hand. A very fine wire was tied to a leg to guide it gently. It landed on her shoulder, and at that moment a slight pull on the wire jerked it into a fatal heart attack. Happily the rest were returned to and released on their home beach. Up on the cliff by the beach there is a tree, also native to California, that is remarkable. At first sight it is quite ordinary, but when one shook it, a cloud of fluttering pale yellow butterflies rose from its umbrella top, hovered over it then slowly settled down again in the foliage. En route who knows where, the butterflies rested in their seasonal migration in this tree, lending it a halo whenever they were stirred.

In the early sixties Big Sur was a center of sorts for writers, painters, and hippies a shade cleaner and better off than the ones in the movement later. Their clothes were a mixture of thrift-shop bargains, garments salvaged from attics, and odds and ends that had caught their fancy. I saw there Mexican sarapes with thirties' satin pajamas, sweat shirts painted with zodiacal signs, feather boas with blue jeans. With their long hair in straight tresses or tousled mops, these men and women started that trend in contemporary fashion.

In the film, Elizabeth was supposed to be one of the tribe. I designed for her a series of ponchos which were becoming and also fitted the hippie scene. The only problem with the costumes in the picture arose in having to transform French extras into Carmel matrons. Often in contemporary films of this kind extras are given an idea of what is needed and use their own clothes. When the call went out for the extras in the country-club scene, it was obvious that not many women in Paris resemble the American country-club type. A few wives of American officials and businessmen in Paris turned up, largely out of curiosity and to be within range of the Burtons. But for the French women who were extras, I had to put together outfits to give the particular American look. I resorted to a shop where American women living in Paris seemed to sell their old clothes, and added to these selections some characteristic hats and other touches.

The Taming of the Shrew brought us back to Rome. First, however, we went to England. Richard appeared in the title role of *Doctor Faustus* in Oxford, with Elizabeth in full beauty as Helen of Troy, though not required to speak. All of us involved in this drama donated our services for the benefit of OUDS (the Oxford University Dramatic Society). In the swim of English classics, Elizabeth tackled Shakespeare with aplomb in Rome. Before *Shrew*, however, she gave what was probably her best performance as the hellion in *Who's Afraid of Virginia Woolf?*

The film was Ernest Lehman's debut as a producer. He also adapted the Edward Albee play. It was also Mike Nichols' first assignment to direct a film. For Elizabeth, it was the first part which did not depend on her looks. She portrayed a woman twelve years older than herself. For me, it was the first time a large number of costumes were not required; there were only four characters in the story, which took place in one long evening and night, mostly in a professor's house on a college campus. Only Elizabeth had a change of clothes in the film.

Before the production started I got a five-page letter from Ernie describing how he thought the four characters should look, though most of it concerned what he thought Elizabeth should wear. He was torn between black velvet with a skirt slit up to her crotch and a shiny brocade number with pants. Mike agreed with me that the character of Martha should look like a slob, her clothes so commonplace that at a glance she was one with the disorder, sloppiness, and indifference that reigned in her house.

I chose suede for the dress she first appeared in because it is a bulky material that tends to make a person appear heavier. Suede also soaks up light on a set so that on film the dress looked dull and tired. For some reason Elizabeth took to riding a bicycle on the lot. Fortunately the stretching of the seat during this unusual exercising added to the forlorn look of the dress. She fell off the bike quite regularly and split the dress right across the behind. Her other outfit was a pair of pants with a badly fitting silk Eisenhower jacket and an American Indian necklace.

The only problem that came up with the clothes in the film was trying to keep Sandy Dennis from looking fat. She played a young, psychopathic wife whose thinness and narrow hips were mentioned throughout the story. After the first week's shooting, Sandy showed unmistakable signs of being pregnant, though she vehemently denied it. I resorted to a short and rather drab squirrel jacket around her shoulders through most of the picture.

While on these productions with Elizabeth there was occasion to wonder about a perennial question of show business: what makes a star?

There are of course many kinds of stars among actors and actresses; there are also a few writers, directors, producers who have star status. Some are confident in their talents; others, gifted, seem either not to get the scripts or to choose poor ones. Some rely on intense press agentry. Indeed, star rank through publicity has spread to almost every field and has become obsessive image-building — conspicuously in politics, sports, fashion. What produces the stars of entertainment seems to depend as much on circumstances and opportunity as on talent and performance; on personality as well as on ambition and drive; above all, on a lot of luck. A fine sense of timing not only in performance but in choosing parts is important. The interest and loyalty of audiences are of course vital. And although the situation has greatly changed since the era of the big studios, each with its luminaries and covey of starlets, stardom is still the goal of performers and the star system is generally considered indispensable.

I caught another clue about stars in films while working with Elizabeth. A star since childhood, she has sustained a long record and despite several quite dismal films continues to interest and attract a worldwide audience. I noticed on the set, even in costume tests, that she has an instinctive rapport with the camera and seems completely at ease, a gift which may partly account for that elusive quality which makes a few stars shine more brilliantly than others.

Broadway has always honored its top stars as much for their drawing power as for their record of performance. Among those on Broadway for whom I designed costumes there were multi-talented stars, some of whom I have already mentioned. Since I worked mainly on musicals, the stars of long standing represent styles of song and characterization familiar to and beloved by their fans: Ethel Merman with her brand of exuberant comedy and the unforgettable brassy volume of voice; Mary Martin, "charm-de-luxe," who gives enormous pleasure to audiences whether through laughter or a pull at the heart strings; Gwen Verdon, the gamine and hoofer, unmatched in her line; Florence Henderson, enchanting in the very demanding role of *The Girl Who Came to Supper,* applauded by the maestro Noel Coward himself for her rendering of the music and lyrics he wrote for this show. In 1967 Leslie Uggams got her chance, perhaps inevitably, in a message musical *Hallelujah, Baby!* through which she acted, sang, and danced with brio, supported by a young spirited company of many talents. It was fun working with them and most of the costumes, contemporary and gay, were executed by the new costume house of Barbara Matera.

Once in a while, a newcomer flashes across the horizon and "a star is born." He or she may become a star — given the right parts, the right plays or films, and with a modicum of luck — and in time join the roster of stars and personalities in entertainment.

In *Funny Girl* Ray Stark brought Barbra Streisand to Broadway and later to the movies. With the tenacity of barracudas both Ray and Barbra hung on to this potential hit for months on the road, through changes in the script, juggling of songs, two directors, and five postponements of the opening night in New York. For their hard work and determination, Ray was well rewarded. This musical, based on his mother-in-law Fanny Brice's earlier years and first successes, was a sensation. Barbra deservedly leapt to stardom and became the new idol of the adolescents.

Barbra had an extraordinary memory about movies and stars. With the strong streak of Walter Mitty in her, she would turn up at fittings impersonating stars, usually of the twenties. The best was when she imagined herself as Garbo, dressed like and giving a full performance of that unique star. She adored clothes and wore them with flair. She liked to vary the size of the padding in her bras, which I found amusing but was maddening to the fitters.

Hollywood was curious about Barbra because for quite a while no new personality had made the impact she had achieved in the play. But they could do little but blink. Barbra with her logorrhea expressed her opinions freely and endlessly about everyone and everything, including the technique of movie making. She told Harry Stradling, one of Hollywood's top cameramen, how to light her, from which angle to aim the camera — in short, how to handle the camera. Having picked up the notion popular at the time among the intellectuals in the business that movies should look "grainy," she went into explicit detail about the French films that were being shown with this artistic effect. She wanted her film to look this way, unaware that it was due to the use of cheap film that the French independents of necessity had to use. After she had finished her explanation and directions, Harry said: "OK Barbra. I'll tell you what we'll do. I'll go ahead and shoot the picture like we usually do, and afterwards we'll scratch up the film for your grainy look."

The brazen assurance was still in full force and even more tiresome in *Hello, Dolly!* It floored the producer Ernie Lehman and intimidated him, to the detriment of the picture. A front and a performance in itself, it must have been exhausting to sustain at the pace and volume Barbra seemed capable of. While we were waiting on the sound stage one day before the shooting of a scene, I asked her why she went on so, as it took so much out of her, to which she explained that she had to suffer to be able to perform.

Elizabeth Taylor as Kate, on the set just before shooting of the wedding scene in *The Taming of the Shrew*.

The shrew in the opening scene. Photograph by Robert Penn.

Headdress of the costume in the Wedding Banquet scene, *The Taming of the Shrew*.

Kate's cloak in Wedding Banquet scene.

Fanny in the scene on returning from the honeymoon trip. Courtesy Ray Stark. Rastar Productions/Columbia Pictures.

Barbra Streisand as Fanny Brice in the opening scene of *Funny Girl*. Courtesy Ray Stark. Rastar Productions/Columbia Pictures.

Barbra clowning on a set of *Hello, Dolly!*
© 1969 Chenault Productions, Inc. and 20th Century-Fox Film Corp. All Rights Reserved.

Dolly in Wedding scene.

15. Justine/The Great White Hope

In common with great numbers of readers, I had been enthralled by Lawrence Durrell's Alexandria Quartet, composed of the novels *Justine, Balthazar, Mountolive, Clea.* Walter Wanger with characteristic deftness had secured the rights to the Quartet even before the complete set had been published. Long before *Justine* went into production, however, Walter's rights had passed to the studio and the script through the typewriters of several writers. To meet the requirements of an average-length movie, the four-volume story was of necessity chopped up. Only the barest story line remained, leaving bewildering gaps and unresolved situations; characters were shorn of motivation, and their conduct became either trivial or eccentric.

The scenes shot on location ideally should have been in Cairo and Alexandria, the home territory of the story. But the Egyptian government forbade it. The way in which movie companies became involved with foreign governments, entangled in national and international red tape, and embroiled with municipal authorities never ceased to be astonishing. There were some odd footnotes. For one, Nasser was a compulsive movie fan, in a position to arrange for almost nightly private screenings of American films (his favorites), yet making *Cleopatra* in Egypt was banned. When the studio was forbidden to shoot scenes there for *Justine* it was decided to go on location to Tunisia on the assumption that it would do just as well: Arabs looked alike, dressed in the same way, and a souk was a souk wherever located — a deplorable notion completely incorrect.

What one sees in the countries and among the peoples of North Africa varies greatly of course; and there is a great difference between Cairo and Alexandria in the thirties — the period of *Justine* — and Tunisia today. In Tunis, the souk is a substantial section of the city with arcades, streets, and alleys of shops; elsewhere in Tunisia souks are just groups of stalls set up outdoors or where the merchandise is spread out on the ground. As to the clothes, the film was mainly about Western characters and Europeanized

Egyptians; but in regard to the people in the background or on the streets in the scenes, there were significant differences.

In Egypt in the thirties men wore the fez. Some wore Western suits, officials often the frock coat, some men preferred a combination of European and Arab clothes, and there were many djellabahs. In Tunis today, as throughout the Arab world, the fez has been largely discarded. One sees more Western clothes. Djellabahs are fewer. Many women in Tunisia still wear the loose white cotton robes that shroud them from head to toe, while the Egyptian women usually wear black. Many of the older women retain the yashmak or veil across the face. Some who no longer veil their faces nevertheless hold a corner of their garment in the mouth, half veiling the face, and when addressed, have a habit of partly covering their faces with a hand.

A few scenes of *Justine* were shot at Cap Bon and at an old fortress on the outskirts of Tunis. Some interior scenes were made in the D'Erlanger villa in Sidi Bou Said — the village of clean white houses, most of them with cerulean blue shutters, where Gide stayed and which he made famous.

A key scene in the film was the masquerade ball. It brought together the principals and certain crucial incidents in the story during the ball. The courtyard of the National Assembly Hall, a pseudo-Arabic black and white marble edifice, served in the film for the setting in Alexandria. During the week of filming the scene, the lights and decorations overhead and around the courtyard had to be removed after each night's shooting since the Tunisian parliament sat during the day.

Evening clothes of the thirties for the hundreds of men and women extras had to be selected and rented from various sources in Hollywood, London, Paris. As the occasion was a masquerade and, as in the book, a domino ball, everyone had also to be covered for the earlier part of the scene in long dominos and half-masks. Since the hundreds of extras' costumes could not be stored in the Assembly building, they were kept in dressing rooms at the Municipal Stadium and trucked back and forth for the scene, which irked Tunisians accustomed to a daily dip in the municipal swimming pool.

There is no doubt that a visiting movie company is a disrupting influence. One should add, the disruption is two-way. But the movies get made, foreign exchange flourishes, governments down to the smallest unit of the bureaucracy and numbers of local citizens benefit. Most of us working abroad learned a lot on and off the job.

Anouk Aimée is a star who projects some of the mystery associated with Garbo. It was perfect casting to choose her for Justine. At the time *Justine* was being prepared, Anouk was working in a French film being made in Hollywood. She was not keen to work for an American studio, nor did she like the idea of an American designer for her clothes. She returned to France, asked that the sketches for her costumes be mailed to Paris for her approval, the clothes be made in Paris, and I should go over to supervise them there. This was a bit too much even for a Hollywood studio used to star stuff. The costumes were started in Hollywood; as other costumes were made in London, Anouk's were finished there. When they were ready, she was taking a breather in Nice, so a fitter and seamstress and I made a quick trip there and back for fittings.

Anouk had ten changes of costume and looked very good in them. Justine in Durrell's story belonged to the international set in Cairo and was presumably interested in clothes and had a sense of style. All the ten outfits were either white, black, or beige. The evening dress she wore at the ball was, however, of a gold material and the domino over it was a deep red.

When the company returned to Hollywood, George Cukor directed the remainder of the picture. Only a director with his long experience could have given the film coherence. He skillfully put the film together by editing and rearranging what had been shot, and incorporated some footage from a TV documentary of the making of the film shot by a French crew.

Among the scenes that remained to be shot was the children's brothel scene in Alexandria. It was one of the deliberately mystifying situations in the book that Justine was looking for a child she had (or wished some of the characters to believe she had), which prompted her in the scene to search the brothel. The once-strong censorship office in Hollywood no longer had as much power as in the past but one of the prohibitions understood, though up till then not spelled out, was that no children should appear as prostitutes in a film. The producer, the art director, and I met in George's office to hear his plan of shooting the scene. He had had a rough sketch made for the set of a hovel with some cubicles around a room. In the sketch there were a few small shadowy figures. Pointing to them, George announced triumphantly, "They will be midgets!" We started to laugh but immediately sensed the difficulties that might arise. "Wait and see," he assured us. "With the scene dimly lit no one will be able to tell they are not children."

Costume for Anouk Aimée in the riding scene, *Justine*.

Justine in black-and-white outfit.

A community of midgets had lived in Hollywood for some years. It had been one place they could find fairly steady employment. But the group had dwindled. The ones who answered the casting director's call were middle-aged men and women who had not worked in films for years. There were far fewer women than men, and one was a grandmother. We had therefore to use both men and women. There was only one nineteen-year-old girl, about four feet six, who could pass for a child. I was stunned. George, undaunted, fell back on the laconic, "Now *you* make them look convincing. Put veils on them!"

Veils seemed unlikely in brothels in Alexandria, especially for children, but who knows? It was not, however, that vital a point. At any rate, veils were the obvious device to cover the ageing faces. I had some cotton djellabahs made in gaudy colors, bleached and patched to look worn, and added headdresses to help hide the faces. The women had heavy breasts which had to be strapped down. I has to ask one man to shave his hands and forearms, which he did not mind doing, but he balked at shedding his large mustache and was persuaded to part with it only after many words appealing to logic and his own good nature. Fortunately, all of them had a sense of humor and were amused by the parts they were playing. Nineteen-year-old Penelope, however, had never been in a film and understandably was the only one embarrassed by appearing in the scene. Even though I had used as much yardage as was feasible and had covered the faces as completely as possible, I asked that the lighting be at the very minimum that technology could achieve. On film the scene was mercifully brief, with no close-ups, and turned out so dimly lit that the midgets did give the impression of being children.

In contrast, the filming on location of *The Great White Hope* called for bright Havana sunlight, though we had to settle for an approximation. The play based on episodes in the life of Jack Johnson, the first Negro to win the world's heavyweight title, had been unable to show the fights on stage. The scenes of the fights were the most conspicuous parts of the film. Some were shot in Globe, Arizona. Since the big fight outdoors in Havana when Johnson lost the title could not be shot in Cuba, it was made in Barcelona. It was more economical there than in California to shoot some of the scenes and to gather the large crowd of extras for the big fight.

I knew next to nothing about prizefights when I started on the picture, but soon discovered that, like all clothes, the boxing rig has a history. Through *Ring* magazine and the Helms Sport Museum in Culver City, I learned about kinds of trunks, shoes, and gloves that were used in Johnson's time. The championship belt was an essential prop. Made of gold and studded with diamonds, these belts are worth the proverbial king's ransom, and the museum was naturally reluctant to let the studio use one. Pete Petersen, the prop man at the studio who had made many items large and small for me executed the belt I drew out for the one presented to the champion — Jack Jefferson in the script. On a wide red, white, and blue ribbon we spaced disks and a plaque of a buckle made of simulated scrolled gold and rhinestones.

The cast of *The Great White Hope* was large. Most of the principals' clothes were men's clothes around 1910 to 1915. James Earl Jones stylishly wore the outfits for Jefferson who was a classy dresser. Jane Alexander, who played the white wife of Jefferson, had about ten changes of costume; one blouse she wore was made out of a tablecloth of fine white linen that came from Austria. By such devices one attempts to get period effects and a period "feel" that can not be done satisfactorily with the synthetic materials now available. The costumes that required the most careful organizing were the clothes for the seven thousand extras.

Three women in the café-opening scene, *The Great White Hope*.

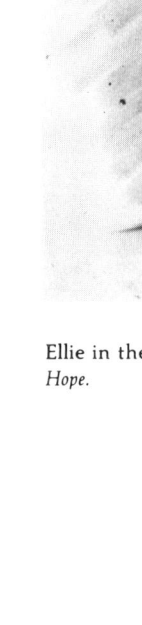

Ellie in the Juarez scene, *The Great White Hope*.

Jane Alexander as Ellie in the Paris scene, *The Great White Hope*.

Johnny de Cuir, the art director on the film, had found a race track in Barcelona; the huge curve of one end of it was converted to serve as the stadium in Havana. To fill this, the thousands of extras were drawn from the usual crowds of applicants and had to be increased by soldiers of a Spanish regiment, the Barcelona Fire Brigade, groups of friends of all of these, and some gypsies from a settlement on the outskirts of Barcelona.

The actual fight in Havana has been well documented. As might be expected in 1915, most of the spectators were men. There was an abundance of women's clothes in the wardrobe department and rental sources from which to make a selection for these extras. The problem was gathering enough clothes for the men not only because of the number, but because Spaniards are generally of smaller build than Americans. However, only those seated near the ring and within camera range had to have period outfits. For a great number of the extras further away we bought garments that had been left unclaimed at laundries and dry-cleaning shops. Those farthest from the ring wore their own trousers and were issued shirts which were bought by the carload from the Salvation Army and thrift shops. Some of the extras had hats — old derbies and caps supplemented by hundreds of plastic "straw" boaters from suppliers of souvenir shops in America. These plastic boaters are still manufactured in quantity for political conventions, rallies, and class reunions. When they were collected at the end of a day's shooting, a number of them had large bites out of the brims. It was suggested that, as they looked like cake, the extras might have thought them good enough to eat, but somebody asked around and was told that the extras just wanted souvenirs.

For this huge crowd I selected a subdued palette of dark gray, brown, ochre, and white — partly to facilitate putting the clothes together, partly to have no colors jumping out from the crowd. Also, the selection was in line with the old photographs of the fight and helped to convey the feel of that period.

Compared to American extras and those in Rome, this Spanish group was docile once they settled in the bleachers. The Spanish soldiers and the Barcelona Fire Brigade marched briskly in formation to their places from the trucks that had brought them, each man clutching the yellow plastic bag of lunch provided by the studio. The minute they sat down they started to nibble, though the fare was dull compared to some of the spreads brought by other extras themselves, who generously offered to share with us the sausages, sardines, anchovies, olives, bread, and wine. There was inevitably a good deal of visiting by friends who were not extras, and we repeatedly had to request through walkie-talkies that the lady in red or the gentleman in the green shirt remove themselves before a shot was made. The first "rushes" of the film shot of this crowd, fortunately not used in the final editing, showed no ladies in red but too many yellow plastic bags which looked as though the men had brought along their laundry.

"Havana" fight scene of *The Great White Hope*, shot in Barcelona. Photograph by Lawrence Schiller.

Seven thousand extras was an unusual number even in the past; it is unlikely that so many at one time will be hired again. Circumstances favorable to making movies abroad have changed, the major studios have gone or are declining, and the Hollywood of the movie heyday no longer exists. Of course films will continue to be made. As a medium, films are unrivaled and their potentialities infinite. Even large-scale productions will be tackled, should a good story turn up. But the trend is toward films made by smaller companies that have a tighter organization and are less hampered by arbitrary decisions from high management.

While the small production company still has to cope with vital economic aspects, it has the inestimable freedom to choose a story from the very wide variety of material available and in making the picture to shoot exteriors in an almost worldwide choice of places and interiors in studios in America and abroad. The story holds the key. "A good story" — and there are endless opinions as to what that is — supersedes the star and all other elements in the making of a film. Costume designing is one cog in the wheel. What makes the wheel go round is the story. Lucky as I have been in the variety and range of opportunities presented in scripts, there have been some lulus and there have been stretches of sameness of story lines and periods. The perennial frustration in movie making is the good story material available, so little of which is tapped.

In theater, as on the screen, the story is of first importance. A straight play cannot survive a weak story. At one time, the story line of a musical could be frail yet acceptable and even welcomed as a vehicle for star, music, pretty numbers — a carefree evening of light entertainment. In many cases the story was implausible, sometimes plain silly, but that was part of the entertainment. The attempts off and on to strengthen the story line of a musical and to handle contemporary problems occasionally succeeds, as for instance in *West Side Story*.

However strong or weak the story, each production in theater or films is nevertheless full of varied opportunities rewarding for the designer beyond the job itself. It is a plus when designs turn out appropriate to the story, near to what began on the drawing board, and contribute to the production as a whole. But there is a lot more. I have found that learning about clothes of various periods and different countries always brings up other aspects to explore. Then there are the places on location: although one works much longer hours and a full week, being off the lot and especially abroad adds new dimensions to eye, ear, and mind. There is, moreover, no end to the experience of color, texture, form. There is no end either to the woes and problems that arise in the costume department; but, as part of the job, smoothing them out is a definite plus. Certainly there is monotony in the pattern of work but it is never dull.

Again, there is no end to the variety of the personalities I have worked with, each of singular interest in one way or another. I have been lucky to have worked with some "greats" on Broadway and in Hollywood — great producers, directors, writers, technicians, as well as great performers — and with many less celebrated whom I would call great for their consistently high standard of work and personal qualities. I have been lucky, too, to have participated since the thirties in some great productions and to have been part of the very great changes that have happened in entertainment. They say (and in show business as elsewhere "they" always are up on everything) that we are now in a transition period. We are of course *always* in a transition period. With the new talent abounding, story material available, and fresh formats which will evolve, show business will surely again and again top itself.

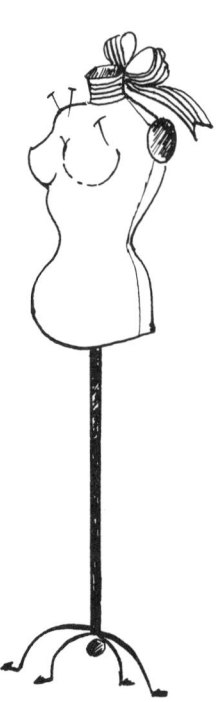

Index

Italic numbers refer to illustrations.

Abbott, George, 27, 30
"Adam and Eve" (*Can-Can*), 95, *97*
Addinsell, Richard, 18
Adiarte, Patrick, 92
Adrian, 58–59, 66
Adrian, Max, 101
Age of Anxiety (ballet), *51*
Aimée, Anouk, 125–126
Albert, Eddie, 44
Alexander, Jane, 127–128, *128*
Alice in Wonderland (play), 18–25, *20-23*, 26, 27
Ames, Preston, 76
American in Paris, An (film), 49, 72–77, *74*, *75*, 78
Andrews, Dana, 68
Arlen, Harold, 76
As Thousands Cheer (revue), 26–27, *28-29*, 43
Astor, Mary, 61, *63*, 64
Ayers, Lemuel, 59

Bailey, Pearl, 94
Bakst, Leon, 30
Balanchine, George, 30, 33
Banjo Eyes (musical), 44
Banton, Travis, 66
Barrymore, Ethel, 24
Bay, Howard, 39
Bemelmans, Ludwig, 67
Benois, Alexandre, 15
Bérard, Christian, 15
Berlin, Irving, 26, 37
Berman Costume Company (London), 92
Bernstein, Aline, 8–11, *9*, 13–14, 24, 27, 67
Bernstein, Leonard, 100, 101
Best Years of Our Lives, The (film), 68
Billion Dollar Baby (musical), 68, *69*
Bishop's Wife, The (film), 68
Bolger, Ray, 30, 33, *35*, 44
Booth, Shirley, 70

"Born in a Trunk" (*A Star Is Born*), 76
Bourgeois Gentilhomme, Le (play), 11, 68
Boys and Girls Together (musical), 44
Boys from Syracuse, The (musical), 44
Brancusi, Constantin, 16
Brice, Fanny, 119
Brigadoon (film), 45
Brooks Costume Company, 86
Brown, Hilyard, 115
Brynner, Yul, 78, 82, *83*, 84, 92
Bufano, Remo, 24
Burton, Richard, 114, 116–117
By the Beautiful Sea (musical), 70
By Jupiter (musical), 44

Calthrop, Gladys, 67
Can-Can (film), *54*, 95, *97-98*, 98–99, 105
Candide (musical), *51*, *55*, 70, 94, 101–104, *103*
Cantor, Eddie, 44
Caron, Leslie, 72, 73, *75*
Carroll, Diahann, 94
Chang, Wah, 95
Cherry Orchard, The (play), 12–13, *13*
Chevalier, Maurice, 95
Civic Repertory Theatre, 8–14, *10*, 15, 18, 24–25, 46
Clark, Bobby, 36, 68
Cleopatra (film), 61, 65, 105–115, *108-111*, *113*, 116, 124
Comden, Betty, 68
Cook, Barbara, 101
Costume Designers' Guild, 67
Coward, Noel, 118
Crawford, Cheryl, 94
Crawford, Joan, 59
Cukor, George, 127

Dandridge, Dorothy, 94
Dassin, Jules, 60
Davis, Sammy, Jr., 94–95

134

De Cuir, John, 92, 105, 129
Dennis, Sandy, 118
Derain, André, 15
Dietrich, Marlene, 60
Doctor Faustus (play), 117
Douglas, Melvyn, 70
Drake, Betsy, 70
Drury Lane Theatre, 42
Dufy, Raoul, 73
Durrell, Lawrence, 124

"Easter Parade" (*As Thousands Cheer*), 27, 28–29, 37, 43
Eaves Costume Company, 27
Edens, Roger, 76
Evans, Maurice, 68
Every Girl Should Be Married (film), 70

Ferber, Edna, 44
Fields, Dorothy, 70
Finnell, Carrie, 37–38
Flower-Drum Song (musical and film), 55, 70
Freed, Arthur, 58, 61, 66, 67, 72, 76
Funny Girl (musical and film), 119, *122*

Garland, Judy, 61, *63*, 76–77
Garson, Greer, 58
Gaynor, Janet, 58
Gershwin, George, 72, 73, 94
Gershwin, Ira, 44, 72, 76, 94, 112
Geva, Tamara, 30, 33, *34*
G.I. Hamlet (play), 68
"Girl on *The Police Gazette*, The" (*Star and Garter*), 37, *40*, 43
Girl Who Came to Supper, The (musical), 54, 118
Goldwyn, Frances, 94–95
Goldwyn, Samuel, 68, 93–95
Gould, Morton, 68
Grant, Cary, 70
Great Waltz, The (musical), 44
Great White Hope, The (film), 54, 127–129, *128*, *130–131*
Green, Adolph, 68
Guthrie, Tyrone, 104
Guys and Dolls (film), 48, 93

Hall, Stanley, 106
Hallelujah, Baby! (musical), 47, *50*, 118–119
Hammerstein, Oscar, 42, 44, 78, 79, 82
Hanfstaengl, Putzi, 15
Happy Hunting (musical), 70
Harrison, Rex, 112–113
Hart, Lorenz, 27, 30, 44
Hart, Moss, 26–27, 44
Hartman, Don, 70
Haslam, Courtney, 107
haute couture (Paris), 16–17
Hellman, Lillian, 101

Hello, Dolly! (film), 119, *123*
Henderson, Florence, 118
Heyward, Du Bose, 94
Hobson, Valerie, 92

I Picked a Daisy (musical), 52

Jones, James Earl, 127
Jourdain, Louis, 95
Jubilee (musical), 44
Juno (musical), 70
Justine (film), 53, 124–127, *126*

Karinska, 40, 101–104
Kaufman, George S., 44
Kaye, Danny, 44, 68
Kelly, Gene, 72, 73, *75*, 76
Kelly, Orry, 66
Kerr, Deborah, 92
Khrushchev, Nikita, 98–99, *98*
King and I, The (film), 51, 53, 81, *83*, 92; (musical), 38, 39, 42, 70, 78–92, *80*, *81*, *85–91*; (musical, London), 42, 92

Lady in the Dark (musical), 44
Land Is Bright, The (play), 44
Lang, Walter, 92, 95
Laurents, Arthur, 100
Lawrence, Gertrude, 44, 78, 83, 84
Lee, Gypsy Rose, 36–37, *40*, 43
Le Gallienne, Eva 8, *9*, 10, 13, 14, *18*, 25
Lehman, Ernest, 117, 119
Lerner, Alan Jay, 72
Levin, Boris, 100
Liliom (play), 24
"Limehouse" (*Ziegfeld Follies*), 67–68
Loy, Myrna, 68

MacCarthy, Agnes, 11
MacLaine, Shirley, 95, 99
Madame Curie (film), 58, 66
Magdalena (musical), 43, 70, *71*
Manet, Édouard, 73
Mankiewicz, Joseph, 93, 105–107, 112
March, Fredric, 68
Martin, Mary, 118
Mason, James, 76
Massine, Léonid, 27
Mata Hari (musical), 45
Matera, Barbara, 119
Mature, Victor, 44
Mayer, Louis B., 58–59
Mayo, Virginia, 68
Me and Juliet (musical), 70
Meet Me in St. Louis (film), 59, 61–64, *62–63*, 66, 76
Meredith, Burgess, 11
Merman, Doc, 61

135

Merman, Ethel, 70, 118
Mielziner, Jo, 30, 78
Minnelli, Vincente, 72
Mongkut, King of Siam, 38; *80*
Moore, Constance, 44
Moreno, Rita, 92

Nasser, Gamal, 124
Nathan, Robert, 60, 68
Nazimova, Alla, 12-13, *12*
Nichols, Mike, 117

Of Thee I Sing (musical), 70
On Your Toes (musical), 27, 30, *31-35*, 45, 55

Pan, Hermes, 95
Pan Am Makes the Going Great (ballet), *48*
Peepshow (revue), 37-39, *41, 42,* 70, 78
Peter Pan (play), 11, 13
Peters, Brock, 94
Petersen, Pete, 127
Petina, Irra, 101
Phumipon Aduldet, King of Thailand, 38-39, 78
Pidgeon, Walter, 58
Porgy and Bess (film), *54*, 93-95, *96*
Porter, Cole, 44
Price, Leontyne, 94
Prowse, Juliet, 95

Reiner, Ethel Linder, 101
Robbins, Jerome, 68, 78, 92, 100
Rodgers, Richard, 27, 30, 33, 42, 44, 78, 82
Romberg, Sigmund, 44
Romeo and Juliet (play), 11-12, 100
Rousseau, Henri, 73
Rounseville, Robert, 101
Rubenstein, Ida, 15

Sandpiper, The (film), 116-117
Saunders, Terry, 92
Savo, Jimmy, 44
Schary, Dore, 76
"Scheherazade" (*On Your Toes*), 30-32, *31, 32, 45*
Schildkraut, Joseph "Pepe," 24
Schwartz, Arthur, 70
Secret Life of Walter Mitty, The (film), 68
Shamroy, Leon, 92
Shangri-La (musical), 70
Short, Hassard, 26-27, *39*, 58
Simmons, Jean, 93, 112
Sinatra, Frank, 95
Skouras, Spyros, 98-99, *98*
"Slaughter on Tenth Avenue" (*On Your Toes*), 30, 33, *34, 35*
Smith, Oliver, 95, 100
Sokolow, Anna, 104

Sondheim, Stephen, 100
Song Is Born, A (film), 68
Sothern, Georgia, 36
Star and Garter (revue), 36-37, *40, 43*
Star Is Born, A (film), 76
Stark, Ray, 119
Stradling, Harry, 119
Streisand, Barbra, 83, 119, *122, 123*
Sweet Charity (musical), *50*
Sunny River (musical), 44

Taming of the Shrew (film), *53*, 116, 117, *120-121*
Taylor, Elizabeth, 65, 105-112, *108-111*, 114-118, *120*
Tchelitchev, Pavel, 15
Tenniel, Sir John, 18-20, *19*, 24
Thaibok, 39, 42
Thompson, James, 39, 78, 82
Throckmorton, Cleon, 24
Thurber, James, 68
Todd, Mike, 36-39, 68
Toulouse-Lautrec, Henri de, 73
"Traviata" (*Ziegfeld Follies*), *56*, 67-68
Tree Grows in Brooklyn, A (musical), 70
Turner, Lana, 60

Uggams, Leslie, *47*, 118
Union: Brotherhood of Painters, Decorators, and Paperhangers of America, 67
Union Pacific (ballet), 27

Van Druten, John, 78, 82
Van Gogh, Vincent, 73
Verdon, Gwen, 118
Venuta, Benay, 44
Villa-Lobos, Hector, 43, 70

Wanger, Walter, 105-107, 112, 114, 124
Wassilichikov, Irina, 107
Weill, Kurt, 44
West Side Story (musical and film), 70, 100-101, *102-103*, 105, 132
White Horse Inn (musical), 44
Who's Afraid of Virginia Woolf? (film), 116-117
Whyte, Jerome, 78, 82
Wilbur, Richard, 101
Wolfe, Thomas, 13
Worth, 13
Would-Be Gentleman, The (play), 68
Wright, Teresa, 68
Wynn, Ed, 44

Yolanda and the Thief (film), 67
Young, Loretta, 68, 112

Ziegfeld Follies (film), *56*, 68
Zimmer, Jessie, 33